# DR. GARY SMALLEY
# TED CUNNINGHAM

# From ANGER to INTIMACY

*How Forgiveness Can Transform Your Marriage*

## Study Guide

**Regal**

**From Gospel Light**
**Ventura, California, U.S.A.**

Published by Regal
From Gospel Light
Ventura, California, U.S.A.
*www.regalbooks.com*
Printed in the U.S.A.

Library of Congress Cataloging-in-Publication Data
Smalley, Gary.
From anger to intimacy. Study guide / Gary Smalley and Ted Cunningham.
p. cm.
ISBN 978-0-8307-4675-0 (trade paper)
1. Marriage—Religious aspects—Christianity. 2. Anger—Religious aspects—Christianity.
3. Forgiveness—Religious aspects—Christianity. I. Cunningham, Ted. II. Title.
BV835.S5524 2009
248.4—dc22
2008023489

1 2 3 4 5 6 7 8 9 10 / 15 14 13 12 11 10 09 08

Rights for publishing this book outside the U.S.A. or in non-English languages are
administered by Gospel Light Worldwide, an international not-for-profit ministry.
For additional information, please visit www.glww.org, email info@glww.org, or write to
Gospel Light Worldwide, 1957 Eastman Avenue, Ventura, CA 93003, U.S.A.

# Contents

# Introduction

The *From Anger to Intimacy Study Guide* is designed to be used in conjunction with the *From Anger to Intimacy* book and DVD. Whether you partake of the study with your spouse, a small group or during a church seminar, we encourage you to share what you're learning with those closest to you! Talk about the questions and Scripture passages with your spouse, friends and any mentors. As you grow closer to God and to your spouse as you work through the study, don't be shy about sharing the good news of what God is doing in your life.

Each section begins with an introductory section, "For Starters," followed by some open-ended questions designed to get the discussion going. After you complete this section, you'll want to watch the DVD and see Gary and Ted share their thoughts and insights on the material. Then, it's time for the main "Study and Discussion." You'll want to keep your Bible nearby. There are lots of great Scriptures and questions to reflect on and discuss. Finally, you'll have the opportunity to put what you are learning into practice by selecting at least one of three "Put It into Practice" options before you begin the next session.

Our hope and prayer for you is that God will use this study to awaken new levels of communication, understanding and forgiveness in your relationship with your spouse and that you will discover the marriage you never thought possible!

# Anger: Stuff, Spew or Study

## Chapters 1–2 in *From Anger to Intimacy*

## For Starters

While I (Ted) have an amazing relationship with my wife, Amy, there are still times when we misunderstand each other. Those moments always lead to tension. Sometimes, particularly if my feelings are hurt, I will express anger. It may be something small like a misunderstanding about something I asked her to do; or worse, something she asked *me* to do, and because of my forgetfulness, I left it undone. In those moments, I am really mad at myself; but all too often the first person I take it out on is my wife.

Over the past few years, both Amy and I have really begun to be students of our anger. We don't want to stuff the anger away, because we know it will rear its ugly head later. And we don't want to spew out awful words that can never be taken back. Instead, we want to live together in a way that is God-honoring and builds each other up. That means that when tensions flare, we need to look at the source of the misunderstanding. We need to look at the circumstances of what caused the situation if we're going to avoid it in the future.

Studying our anger has been one of the most powerful tools that Amy and I have used in our marriage to build intimacy. It has forced us to examine our hearts. Instead of spending our time and energy stuffing anger or spewing it, we focus on studying it and finding a solution. Why does this matter so much? Because stuffing or spewing anger is a waste of emotional, mental and spiritual energy. These reactions open the door of our hearts to unhealthy things like unforgiveness, bitterness and cynicism. And those are doors that all of us should keep shut.

When anger grips either Amy's or my heart, it causes us to step away from each other and feel disconnected; this naturally undermines the intimacy of our relationship. That's why I need to be proactive to study and prayerfully consider what causes our anger. We want to feel close to each other and have the best possible marriage. We have a hunch that you do too! That's why, over the course of this study, we'll help you dive into the issue of anger and how you can resolve conflicts and tensions in your marriage relationship.

Think of several small things people can do that get on your nerves. In the space below, make a list of three pet peeves.

_____

_____

_____

_____

Now take a moment to study the pet peeves you listed. Why do these specific things bother you? Is there a history or background story to why they are bothersome? Explain.

_____

_____

_____

_____

How does listening to your spouse's pet peeves and the reasons behind them, and your spouse's listening to your pet peeves, help you both feel more understood? Why is understanding each other so important for a healthy relationship?

_____

_____

_____

_____

# Introduction to DVD

Everyone experiences anger from time to time; anger is a God-given emotion. It's even possible for anger to be expressed for healthy reasons. To know the difference between healthy anger and unhealthy anger, you need to study it. In this first lesson, we'll explore how anger is a secondary emotion, not a primary one. You'll begin to discover how you can better deal with the anger that pops up in your own marriage and life. Let's watch as Gary and Ted introduce this idea.

# Discussion and Study

It's important to recognize that anger in and of itself is not a bad thing. Anger is a God-given, God-designed emotion. In fact, God feels anger too! But what you do with your anger determines its impact on your spiritual, mental and emotional health.

Can you think of any situations in which anger is a healthy response?

_____

_____

_____

_____

_____

_____

_____

_____

One healthy expression of anger is toward evil. If you cannot feel anger toward evil, then it stands to reason that you do not love what is good. In other words, there are some things that it's okay to get angry about, like oppression of people and injustice.

## Nehemiah's Righteous Anger

This kind of anger was demonstrated in the life story of Nehemiah. As he listened to the outcry of the Jewish people, he learned about the oppression of the land and how usury—exorbitant interest rates on borrowed money—was taking a toll on the community.

Read Nehemiah 5:1-6. What was the situation that made Nehemiah angry?

_____

_____

_____

_____

_____

What did his emotional response cause Nehemiah to do? (See Nehemiah 5:7-11.)

_____

_____

_____

_____

What was the outcome of Nehemiah's righteous response? (See Nehemiah 5:11-13.)

_____

_____

_____

_____

_____

God wants you to be angry about some things, like social injustice, because He feels the anger too. But even when you get upset about good, righteous, helpful, constructive causes, you still must deal with your anger in an appropriate way and let your actions and attitudes be bathed in love.

Anger is a secondary emotion. If you stop and think about it, anger is a result, not a cause, of being upset. The causes of anger lie below the surface. (In upcoming pages, we'll refer to these as "buttons" that get pushed.) Take a look at the list of words below and place a check mark by the ones that lead you to feel angry. Then circle the top three sources that are most likely to make you angry.

**Primary Sources of Anger**

I get angry when I feel . . .

____ Abandoned

____ Belittled

____ Cheated

____ Controlled

____ Devalued

____ Disconnected

____ Disrespected

____ Like a failure

____ Inferior

____ Invalidated

____ Judged

____ Neglected

____ Unloved

____ Worthless

Why do you think some of these feelings are more likely than others to lead you to anger?

_____

_____

_____

_____

_____

How can recognizing these hot spots in your emotional life help you prevent yourself from becoming angry?

_____

_____

_____

_____

_____

Are there any other under-the-surface hot spots not listed that lead you to anger? If so, explain.

_____

_____

_____

_____

_____

When any of those feelings are planted in your heart and watered over time, they become like living seeds. They sprout roots and grow until they blossom into anger. Now anger is like a wild weed that produces poison. Eventually it will kill and destroy everything in its path.

## The Lessons of Cain

One of the first people in the Bible to let anger get the best of him was Cain. The book of Genesis tells the story of two brothers, Cain and Abel. By their very nature they were different from each other. Abel kept the flocks while Cain tilled the ground. Both Cain and Abel brought gifts to the Lord representing what they did. Abel offered the Lord one of his flock while Cain brought a harvest offering.

Read Genesis 4:4-5. What was the Lord's response to each of the offerings?

_____

_____

_____

_____

_____

According to Genesis 4:5, what was Cain's emotional response to the situation?

_____

_____

_____

_____

_____

Reflecting on the list of "Primary Sources of Anger," what feeling(s) below the surface do you think was connected to Cain's anger?

_____

_____

_____

_____

What was the Lord's response and encouragement to Cain? (See Genesis 4:5-7.)

_____

_____

_____

_____

What can be learned from Genesis 4:6 about dealing with anger?

_____

_____

_____

_____

Unfortunately, anger got the best of Cain. What did Cain do in Genesis 4:8?

_____

_____

_____

_____

In what ways in your own life have you seen anger lead to "death"?

_____

_____

_____

_____

Like Cain, you may have an encounter or event in your life that produces an emotion leading to an anger response. If you feel wronged or overlooked or unfairly treated, anger will often surface. When the anger is left unresolved, it festers inside of you like an infection until it eventually leads you to sin. That's why it's so important to deal with (to study) the source event and resulting anger before it leads to sin or further self-destructive behavior.

Anger may be taking a bigger toll on your relationships than you realized. It looks something like this:

$$Event \rightarrow Emotion \rightarrow Anger \rightarrow Sin$$

In what ways have you seen this pattern manifest itself in your own life?

_____

_____

_____

_____

_____

_____

What processes or steps do you currently have in place that allow you to be angry without sinning?

_____

_____

_____

_____

_____

_____

In my own life and marriage, I (Ted) have noticed that I have certain buttons that when pushed cause me to get upset and feel angry. Some of my hot buttons are common to most men and include:

- I do not like to feel controlled.
- I do not want to be judged.
- I do not want to feel like a failure.

My wife's hot buttons are common to most women and include:

- I do not want to feel disconnected.
- I do not want to feel rejected.

Reflecting on this list, which of these are hot buttons for you? Which of these are hot buttons for your spouse?

_____

_____

_____

_____

Do you or your spouse have a hot button that is not listed? If so, explain.

_____

_____

_____

_____

These hot buttons are important to recognize, because when you know your own buttons, as well as those of your spouse, then you can avoid pressing them unintentionally. You can also learn how to respond in a more healthy way in any given situation.

## Stuff, Spew and Study

There are three primary responses to anger. You can *stuff it*. You can *spew it*. You can *study it*.

I'd love to tell you that I naturally study my anger so that it doesn't get the best of me; but the truth is that by nature I tend to stuff my anger. I pack it away where it can grow roots.

I grew up in a church that taught you that you never quite measure up and God never loves you until you do enough certain things. As a result, I learned to respond more quietly. While I would not outwardly be angry, I would harbor resentment and unforgiveness. This unhealthy pattern followed me right into my marriage.

Whenever one of my hot buttons gets pushed, my reactions include:

- Withdrawal
- Defensive Posture
- Sarcasm

Sometimes my lower lip starts quivering. My statements become short and barbed. When you see me take a defensive position in thought, word and posture, then you know one of my hot buttons has been pushed, and as much as I try to stuff it, I really can't hold it in. Eventually, the anger will emerge with destruction in its wake. That's one reason the Bible gives specific instructions for stuffers.

*I (Ted) secretly hope that if I don't deal with something, then it will magically go away. Though I know intellectually that unresolved issues never just go away, I still find myself tempted to stuff issues.*

Read Ephesians 4:26. In what ways does this verse specifically address those who are prone to stuffing?

_____

_____

_____

_____

_____

What advice does the verse give on dealing with anger?

_____

_____

_____

_____

_____

In what ways have you found this verse to offer wisdom and truth in your own life?

_____

_____

_____

_____

_____

_____

In what ways is this verse particularly vital to the health of a marriage relationship?

_____

_____

_____

_____

_____

## You Can Spew It

If you aren't a stuffer, then there's a good chance that you're prone to spewing anger. That means that you allow your emotions to get the best of you and literally spew out anger verbally, emotionally or physically. Spewing anger will undermine all of your relationships. Spewing anger on a spouse can destroy a marriage. Spewing anger on a coworker or friend can undermine a healthy work environment and relationship. Spewing anger on a child can do incredible harm.

All too often, those who spew anger will find someone to agree with them. They'll find someone who will affirm their unhealthy anger or attitude. Unfortunately, what happens is that spewers tend to spread the anger and unforgiveness. The reasoning becomes something like, "Because my best friend was offended, I will not shop there anymore either." Or, "Because my best friend was done wrong, I will treat them as though the offense was committed against me." Thus, spewing anger can infect others.

*Can you think of someone you have struggled with because he (she) is constantly angry? Do you go out of your way to avoid contact with him (her)? Do you feel like you have to walk on eggshells when you're with this person? Do you fear for your own safety or the safety of your family when you're with the person? If so, he (she) probably spews anger and has probably filled his (her) anger bucket almost full.*

Read Proverbs 29:22. In what ways have you seen this verse apply in your own life? In your marriage? In your workplace?

_____

_____

_____

_____

_____

_____

King Nebuchadnezzar was a colorful leader known for many things; one of them was his temper. In Daniel 3, we read that the king made an image of gold that was 90 feet high and 9 feet wide. He commanded that whenever the sound of music played, everyone had to bow down and worship this golden image. Whoever refused would be thrown into a burning furnace. But there were three men in the kingdom who did not obey the king's command.

Read Daniel 3:7-23. What are the names of the three men who refused to bow? (See Daniel 3:12.)

_____

_____

_____

_____

_____

What was King Nebuchadnezzar's attitude when he learned of the three men? (See Daniel 3:13,19.)

_____

_____

_____

_____

_____

Do you think King Nebuchadnezzar is best described as one who stuffs, spews or studies anger? Why?

_____

_____

_____

_____

_____

How did the three men who did not bow down respond to King Nebuchadnezzar's anger in Daniel 3:16-18?

_____

_____

_____

_____

_____

In what ways was the response of the three men in Daniel 3:16-18 a model of how to respond when you are faced with an angry person?

_____

_____

_____

_____

_____

## You Can Study It

Rather than stuff or spew your anger, I would highly encourage you to choose a third healthy option: Study it!

When the emotion of anger arises, it's essential to make sure that you respond to God rather than react to people or a given situation. That may mean taking a moment or two to pray before responding; or excusing yourself from the person's presence for a few minutes to regain your composure. It may mean holding your tongue until you have time to objectively process your thoughts about a situation.

Studying your anger and becoming a master of it rather than being mastered by it is one of the true marks of maturity of a follower of Christ and one that I am still learning. I want to become a master student of anger so that I understand where it's coming from and how to respond in a godly, good way, rather than a harmful, destructive way.

====

*Anger has three outlets: You can stuff it. You can spew it. Or you can choose a third option: You can study it. I am convinced that this is God's design for putting an end to unresolved anger. In fact, I believe that it is a spiritual discipline to get angry over the right things and act accordingly.*

====

Now, certain situations, words and responses are going to naturally push your hot buttons. So the question is not if your buttons are going to get pushed, but how will you respond?

Jesus said we will be known as followers of Him by the way we love each other. It's not by the knowledge we have or the number of cans we bring to the local food pantry. While knowing the Scriptures and caring for the poor are important ingredients of being a follower of Christ, ultimately the most important thing is love. When two people are operating in a spirit of love and forgiveness in a marriage relationship, those around them cannot help but notice.

One of the most beautiful displays of forgiveness in the midst of injustice is demonstrated in the story of Stephen. In Acts 7, he boldly preached the good news of Jesus Christ, but the response of the audience was anything but kind.

Read Acts 7:54-60. What was the response of the listeners to Stephen's words? (See Acts 7:54,57-58.)

_____

_____

_____

_____

_____

What was Stephen focused on during this difficult time? (See Acts 7:55-56.)

_____

_____

_____

_____

What was Stephen's response to the anger being spewed verbally and physically? (See Acts 7:60.)

_____

_____

_____

_____

_____

Please understand that if you're in an abusive relationship or situation, you need to get help. Abuse is never acceptable in a marriage relationship. But the beauty of Stephen's story is found in his attitude of love and forgiveness toward his accusers. His story reminds us that even in the toughest of situations, we can still choose to love and forgive; and by doing so, we glorify God.

## Taking It with You

Everyone will encounter situations that will make him or her angry. The question is, what will you do with your anger? Where will you allow your anger to take you? Or will you take control of your anger?

# Event ➤ Emotion ➤ Anger ➤ Sin

You have three choices when it comes to anger. You can *stuff* it, *spew* it or *study* it. By studying your anger and understanding your hot buttons, you can be better prepared to diffuse anger before it gets the best of you.

## Put It into Practice

Choose at least one of these suggested activities to complete over the next week. Consider sharing with your friends or small-group members the impact it has on you and your relationship with your spouse.

### 1. Study Your Hot Buttons

Make a list of your top hot buttons. Now reflect on any areas of tension, anger or frustration in your life during the past week. Which of your buttons were being pushed in those moments? Over the next seven days, study the moments when your temper flares. Take a step back from the situation and identify which button is being pushed. If appropriate, gently try to explain to the person involved why the situation is making you upset.

## 2. Study Yourself and Your Spouse

Do you tend to stuff or spew? Sit down with your spouse and talk about each of your personal tendencies. What are some specific ways you can hold each other accountable so that you don't stuff or spew? Are there certain phrases or key words you can use to diffuse an angry moment and challenge each other to resist the temptation to stuff or spew? Over the course of the next week, look for opportunities to use these gentle phrases to hold each other accountable.

## 3. Study Your Anger

Take some time with your spouse in a relaxed, nonthreatening environment where you can talk about some of the common situations that frustrate you both. Are there any themes or patterns? How can you work toward a solution rather than against each other?

# Personal Responsibility and Emotions

*Chapters 3–5 in From Anger to Intimacy*

## For Starters

I (Ted) don't know if your wife has ever done this to you, but my wife, Amy, will be driving down the road with me a couple of times a week and look over at me and ask, "What are you thinking about right now?"

If you ever want to know if the guy is thinking about the relationship, know this: He's not! Just kidding. (Well, sort of.) This may seem strange for some women to read, but there are a lot of times when your husband isn't thinking anything at all. His mind is truly blank. I know that in my own life I often find myself thinking about nothing at all.

It's usually at those moments that Amy will ask, "What are you thinking?"

All too often, I'll respond with something truly profound, "We need an oil change in about 600 miles."

That's when she'll gently press, "No, what do you think about our relationship?"

In those moments, I'm reminded of one of her core desires, which is one of the core desires of many women: *connectedness*.

Both men and women have hot buttons that invariably lead to anger. In a marriage relationship, one of the most common hot buttons for women is a feeling of disconnection, while one of the most common hot buttons for men is the feeling of being controlled.

Why is understanding these buttons so important to your marriage? Because when you recognize your main hot button, you can take the necessary steps to diffuse anger and reestablish connectedness in a healthy relationship. In the process, you can learn to take personal responsibility for your actions and learn how to nurture not only your own emotions but also the emotions of your spouse. The result is a life-infused, joy-filled marriage relationship.

On a scale of 1 to 10, how important is it for you to feel connected to your spouse?

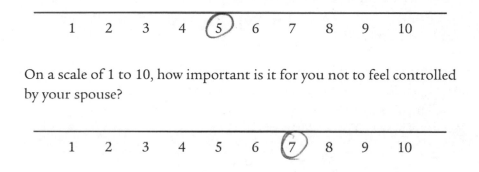

On a scale of 1 to 10, how important is it for you not to feel controlled by your spouse?

What attitudes, actions and behaviors undermine your ability to establish connectedness? What steps do you need to make to change?

_____

_____

_____

_____

_____

# Introduction to DVD

As we've discovered, every man and woman will encounter situations that make them angry. This began in the Garden of Eden and will continue for as long as we are in this world. The question is what will you do with *your* anger? Where will you allow your anger to take you? Or will you take control of your anger? In this second lesson, we'll explore some of the basic needs of both men and women in a marriage and how meeting these needs can diffuse anger and invite forgiveness and love into the relationship. Let's watch as Ted and Gary introduce this idea.

# Discussion and Study

Our friends at the National Institute of Marriage, led by Drs. Greg Smalley and Bob Paul, have done significant research into the hot buttons of couples and how men and women can intervene before harmful, unresolved anger is released in a relationship.

Consider the following patterns that can lead to an anger response. As you read through this progression, can you identify a scenario in your own marriage that starts with hurt, progresses to want and fear, and results in anger?

### 1. You Hurt

A wide range of emotions surface whenever you are wounded, including anger, confusion, worry, rage, frustration, horror and embarrassment. These can often feed off of each other and lead to more anger.

### 2. You Want

When you're hurt, you want to find a solution that will fix the situation and make you feel better. The result is unmet expectations. You may think, "If only my spouse would (fill in the blank)." Any time you put your expectations for rescue in the wrong place, you will be disappointed, which further fuels the hurt and anger.

### 3. You Fear

Whenever a conflict causes powerful emotions of hurt, it stirs specific fears. You may fear that you're not smart enough, competent enough, attractive enough or good enough. The fear only fuels the cycle of anger.

### 4. You React

In order to handle a situation, you fall into well-worn patterns of reacting when someone pushes one of your fear buttons. Rather than base your reactions in love, they are found in an unhealthy pattern of response that often fuels more anger.

## Call a Time-out

The good news is that you can break out of an unhealthy pattern of response. One of the best ways to diffuse anger in a sticky situation is to call a time-out. Sometimes that means putting yourself in time-out so that you don't say something you wish you could take back.

This isn't just a good idea; it's also a biblical idea.

Read James 1:19-20. What specific instruction is given in this passage regarding the response time to a situation?

_Quick to listen, slow to speak, and slow to_
_anger._

Read Proverbs 21:23. In what ways have you found this verse to be true in your marriage?

_Pick your issue's_
_God spoke and created everything Good_
_what do we created when we speak._

Read Proverbs 14:17. What are some of the dangers of being quick-tempered rather than self-controlled?

_You says things that can be hurtful/ our_
_incent anger._

## Turn to God

In addition to calling a time-out, it's important to turn to God when you're tempted with anger or dealing with a frustrating situation. God is always available through prayer, and He is the one you should cry out to first!

King David demonstrated what it looks like to have an open and honest relationship with God throughout the book of Psalms. Whatever difficult situation he was facing, he cried out to God. He didn't hold back. Often within a single psalm we see the change that takes place in David's heart. The focus shifts from the current situation to God's goodness and greatness.

Read Psalm 70. What is David's request to God regarding his enemies? (See vv. 1-3.)

To be brought back to there shame, dishorned

What is David's request to God for those who are faithful? (See v. 4.)

Come quickly to him

What is David's request to God regarding himself in verse 5?

**The steps to receive God's love and power:**

1. Father God, I confess (admit) that I have been grafted into all of the wrong things, parents, society's beliefs and ways, friends and all other influences up to this point today. I confess that I only want Your beliefs controlling me, and I only want You to be my God. I want to abide in Your vine, Jesus, from now on.

2. I repent by cutting myself off right now from the things that I have been wrongly abiding in. I feel myself falling to the ground.

3. By Your "grace," You are lifting me up and carrying me to the Vine, because I admit that I am weak, helpless and "poor in spirit." You, God, are inserting me within the Vine and using Your sap to seal me for eternity, giving me Your life juices of love and changing me with all of Your other characteristics now and forever more.

4. With Your power, God, running through my veins, I will use that power to listen to You by hiding Your "key" words within my heart. I will graft Your words upon my own heart so that I think, speak and act like You. I don't live anymore, but my new life is hidden in You, by faith, and "the life that I now live, I live by the Son of God who loves me and gave Himself for me." Then, I will have Your beliefs and Your ways showing within me as a light to the world.

Why do you think it was important for David to cry out to God in these moments rather than take matters into his own hands? How are the psalms a reminder to you to cry out to God, no matter what the situation?

_____

_____

_____

_____

_____

## Commit to Forgive

As you place your concerns, fears and the weight of the situation before the Lord, there comes a point when you need to make a decision to commit to forgiving your mate no matter what he or she may have done. Now that's not always easy, but there is no better character attribute to have within your very make-up as a Christian than forgiveness. It is the highest quality and the greatest attribute that God has, which stems from His love for us.

That's one reason Ephesians 4:31-32 advises, "Get rid of all bitterness, rage and anger, brawling and slander, along with every form of malice. Be kind and compassionate to one another, forgiving each other, just as in Christ God forgave you."

When you forgive someone, you are expressing the reality that you have been forgiven by God. One of the parables in the Bible that powerfully demonstrates the importance of forgiveness is the story of the unmerciful servant. In Matthew 18, Peter asks Jesus a profound question: "How many times should I forgive my brother when he sins against me?" Peter knows from his rabbinic studies that if a man commits an offense three times, he is to be forgiven; but on the fourth, he does not have to be forgiven. Thinking that he was being generous, Peter asks if he should forgive up to seven times.

Jesus responds with an outrageously generous answer: "I tell you, not seven times, but 77 times!" Then Jesus illustrates His point with a story of a king who wanted to settle accounts with his servants. A man who owed 10,000 talents (a LOT of money) was brought before the king. Unable to pay, he and his family were sold. In essence, they were sentenced to slavery.

The man fell on his knees and begged the king for patience. If only he were given more time, he would pay back every last penny. The king forgave the debt, and the man went free. So watch the turn of this story. This guy just got a debt completely wiped out that he could not possibly pay back. His wife and children, who were about to be sold off to pay back the debt, were free as well. He has to be feeling really good, right? What do you think the attitude of this guy should be? Generous, right? But when a fellow servant who owed him a mere 100 denari came to beg for more time to pay, the man grabbed him and began strangling him, all the while demanding, "Pay me what you owe me!"

The fellow servant issued a familiar cry: "Be patient with me, and I will pay you back."

Those words should have jogged the guy's memory. It was the very same request he had made of the king. But he refused to give leniency and had the man who owned him a pittance thrown into prison.

When the king heard the story, he called the servant whose debt he had forgiven into his chambers.

Read Matthew 18:32-34. What was the outcome of the story?

Tortured until he paid it back

Read Matthew 18:35. Why did Jesus tell this story? What message was He trying to convey?

How does knowing how much you have been forgiven by God help you extend forgiveness to others? To your spouse?

_____

_____

_____

_____

## Choose a Different Reaction

Another tactic for diffusing anger is to choose a different reaction. That means breaking out of the script you may have unknowingly been using. Instead of falling back on your standard reply, think of something fresh, new and full of love. Rather than shut down and say, "I don't want to talk about this right now," ask for a few minutes to gather your thoughts and let your spouse know that you want to work things through. Instead of reacting in anger, look for opportunities to tame the situation with reminders like, "We're going to get through this"; "Even right now, I still love you more than you could know"; and "Never forget that we're on the same team."

In John 13, we read of the final meal Jesus shared with His disciples. Several unexpected things were about to happen.

According to John 13:2-3, what was already happening in Judas's heart?

Giving into evil

_____

_____

_____

_____

Though Jesus could have been angry with Judas, how does Jesus respond to Judas and all of the disciples? (See John 13:1-11.)

_____

_____

_____

_____

In what ways is Jesus' response surprising or unexpected?

_____

_____

_____

_____

_____

Read John 13:12-17. What are Jesus' specific instructions?

To treat has each other as he treated
them

_____

_____

_____

How does serving and loving one another diffuse anger within a marriage?

_____

_____

_____

_____

What is your emotional reaction to being served and loved uncondi-tionally?

_____

_____

_____

_____

## Create Judgment-Free Zones

Finally, when diffusing anger, it's important to create judgment-free zones. Those are places where you can honestly communicate in the safety of a loving relationship. That means you can't shut down. You can't spew. You have to play fair and keep your heart open.

Here is what I (Ted) used to do in my marriage. I would get mad at Amy and I would close my heart and go into the basement. I would wait for her to come down and say, "Ted, I'm sorry."

Then I would say, "That's good. Do you have anything else to say?"

She would say, "I shouldn't have said those words."

I used to think that it was her responsibility to keep my heart open and create a judgment-free zone. I used to think that if she said the right things and I reacted well to them, then I would have an open heart and we would continue to live in peace. What I didn't realize is that I was expressing conditional love, not the unconditional love that God calls us to show each other as followers of Jesus.

Over the years, I've discovered that it takes both spouses to create a judgment-free zone where both are fully engaged and can communicate freely. Creating a judgment-free zone is really a heart issue.

Read Ephesians 4:2. In what ways does abiding by this verse help create a judgment-free zone?

You show humility and love

_____

_____

_____

_____

What steps can you take in your own marriage to create a judgment-free zone?

_____

_____

_____

_____

## Nurturing Your Emotions

In addition to taking personal responsibility for your reactions, it's also important to nurture your emotions. Now, some people try to dismiss emotions as unimportant, but if you want to get a grip on destructive anger or any other unhealthy emotion in your life, then you need to look for ways to nurture the healthy emotions in your life.

One of the keys to nurturing your emotions is to realize that as you think in your heart, so you are. Scientists have proved that there is a significant link between the heart and mind. In fact, studies show that the brain communicates with the heart and the heart communicates with the brain. At times, the heart can override the brain. Why is this so important?

In Psalm 139:23, David cries out, "Search me, O God, and know my heart; test me and know my anxious thoughts." In other words, we need to look inside our own hearts, because that's where some of our anxious thoughts and other unhealthy thoughts come from. And we need God to give us a right and healthy perspective.

Read Philippians 4:8-9. What does this passage encourage us to focus our hearts and minds on? How does focusing on these things change your attitude, actions and perspective?

positive and loving things, God honering and
God gloify. Dont dwell on negative thing

One very practical way to nurture your emotions and focus your heart and mind on things that build yourself and others up is to study Scripture.

Read Psalm 119:11. What is one of the direct benefits of storing up God's Word in your heart?

you will sin less to God

Read Colossians 3:16. What are some practical ways that you can incorporate the reading of Scripture, praise and worship into your everyday life?

listening to christian music

_____

_____

_____

_____

Pray for dennis and his daughter that he may come to you in his last days.

## The Emotional Aftershock and Taking Every Thought Captive

You may have an emotional reaction to an event, interaction or situation, but that emotional reaction is usually temporary and short-lived. The real emotional legacy is established in how you respond to the situation—something called the emotional aftershock. When you choose to wallow in unhealthy emotions, you will find your mind stained with bitterness, resentment and anger. But if you learn to respond in a healthy manner, you will find yourself with peace, hope and joy.

Read 2 Corinthians 10:3-5. What are the "strongholds" listed in this passage? (See v. 4.)

_____

_____

_____

_____

_____

How have you seen these "strongholds" try to take hold in your own thought life? In your marriage?

_____

_____

_____

_____

_____

Why is it important to get rid of any bitterness, resentment or anger before it takes root in your life?

_____

_____

_____

_____

_____


## You Are 100 Percent Responsible

Responsibility is hard for many people. But when you take responsibility for your actions and attitudes, you'll actually find a greater level of freedom in your life. When you take responsibility, your relationships become healthier, your grace for others increases and joy can't help but spring up in your heart as you mature in Christ.

God can do amazing things in our life when we take responsibility for our actions and attitudes. We open the door for God to deal with us one on one and bring us into the fullness of who He has created us to be.

One woman who took responsibility for her actions is found in the Gospel of Luke. Read Luke 8:43-49. What did the woman do to Jesus? Why do you think she did it?

_____

_____

_____

_____

_____

What was Jesus' response? (See vv. 45-46.)

_____

_____

_____

_____

_____

How did the woman take personal responsibility for her actions? (See v. 47.)

_____

_____

_____

_____

_____

What was Jesus' response to her taking responsibility? (See v. 48.)

_____

_____

_____

_____

Can you think of a time when you took personal responsibility and found that God met you in a special way at that place? If so, describe.

_____

_____

_____

_____

In this story, Jesus' final words to the woman are simply, "Go in peace." In what ways does taking responsibility invite peace into your life?

_____

_____

_____

_____

## Access to Love, Peace and Hope

Another aspect of nurturing your emotions is recognizing that you have access to love, peace and hope as a child of God. If you have turned your life over to Jesus Christ, He offers you love, peace and hope that the world can never match.

Read John 13:1. How is God's love expressed in this verse?

_____

_____

_____

_____

_____

Read John 15:9. What invitation is issued regarding the love of God?

_____

_____

_____

_____

_____

Read John 14:27. What gift does Jesus offer in this verse?

_____

_____

_____

_____

_____

Read Philippians 4:7. What role can the peace of God play in your life?

_____

_____

_____

_____

_____

Read Hebrews 11:1. How are hope and faith fused?

_____

_____

_____

_____

_____

Read 1 Corinthians 13:7. How are hope and love fused?

_____

_____

_____

_____

_____

## Speak Honorable Words

When you use encouraging, edifying words, you can speak hope and life and love into your marriage relationship.

Read 1 Corinthians 13:1-3. Why is bathing your words in love so important?

_____

_____

_____

_____

Read Galatians 5:22-23. How can this be a grid for the words you speak to your spouse?

_____

_____

_____

_____

## Celebrate the Trials

It's also important to celebrate the trials and joy that will soon come as you grow and mature into who God has called and created you to be. Whenever your buttons get pushed, you need to stop, call a time-out, cry out to God, examine the log in your own eye and start to be thankful. Be grateful that God brought your mate into your life. Do you know what your mate is? Your mate is your number-one partner in helping you figure out how to deal with the snake pit of anger in your life. That is because when your mate frustrates you, it is typically in the areas in which you are identical to him (her). There are things my spouse does that make me snap. Those incidents expose something that God wants to deal with in my heart, not hers, and I am learning to be grateful for those times.

Read Hebrews 12:6-11. What is the purpose of godly discipline in your life? (See Hebrews 12:7-8.)

_____

_____

_____

_____

_____

What are some of the fruit or benefits of being disciplined by God? (See vv. 10-11.)

_____

_____

_____

_____

_____

## Boast in Your Weakness

Boasting in your weakness is another great way to nurture your emotions. It erases false pretenses and expectations, allowing you to be yourself and allowing God to be glorified through you.

Read 2 Corinthians 12:9-10. Why did Paul boast in his weaknesses?

_____

_____

_____

_____

_____

What was accomplished through such boasting?

_____

_____

_____

_____

_____

How does being honest about your weaknesses and faults help you connect with your spouse?

_____

_____

_____

_____

_____

_____

_____

## Taking It with You

When you consider the sources of anger in your life, those hot buttons that are easily pressed, then you are better able to diffuse anger early on in a situation or conversation. Simple activities like taking a time-out, turning to God, committing to forgive and developing a different reaction can go a long way to building and maintaining a healthy relationship with your spouse. In addition, it's important to nurture your emotions. How do you do it? By accepting personal responsibility for your actions and attitudes; by guarding your heart against bitterness; by studying God's Word and focusing on things that are good and real and true and beautiful; by praying to God for strength and accessing the peace, hope and love available to you as God's child; by speaking honorable words, celebrating trials, boasting in your weaknesses. All these and more can go a long way to helping you diffuse anger in your marriage and any other relationship.

# Put It into Practice

Choose at least one of these suggested activities to complete over the next week. Consider sharing with your friends or small-group members the impact it has on you and your relationship with your spouse.

## 1. Take the "Are You a Replayer?" Quiz

Check out pages 102-103 of *From Anger to Intimacy*.

Did anything surprise you about your responses to the test?

_____

_____

_____

_____

_____

_____

_____

Did anything surprise you about your spouse's responses?

_____

_____

_____

_____

_____

_____

How does taking the "Are You a Replayer?" quiz help you better understand yourself? Understand your spouse?

_____

_____

_____

_____

_____

_____

_____

### 2. Know Your Anger Cycle

On page 68 of *From Anger to Intimacy,* Ted provides a diagram of the cycle of anger in marriage. Using the same image, fill in the cycle of anger you experience in your own marriage. What do you have in common with Ted and Amy? What unique challenges do you face as a couple? How does recognizing the cycle help you and your spouse break out of it?

# AMY AND TED'S BUTTONS

**When Ted feels . . .**

**Controlled**

**Judged**

**Like a failure**

**He then . . .**

**Escalates—raises her word count**

**Exaggerates–using "always" and "never"**

**Creates negative beliefs—
assigns motives to actions**

**Withdraws from the conversation**

**Defends his opinions**

**Gets sarcastic**

**When Amy feels . . .**

**Disconnected**

**Abandoned**

**Rejected**

**She then . . .**

## 3. Reflect on Scripture

Reflecting on the Scripture studied throughout this lesson, did you notice a passage of Scripture that gripped your heart or illuminated something new about you or your marriage? If so, consider committing that Scripture to memory over the next week.

# The Spirit of Forgiveness

Chapter 6 in *From Anger to Intimacy*

The Song of Solomon is a beautiful love story. Throughout this romantic book of the Bible, we see a man and woman interacting emotionally, physically and spiritually. In the second chapter, there is a verse that has always caught my attention. Song of Solomon 2:15 says, "Catch for us the foxes, the little foxes that ruin the vineyards, our vineyards that are in bloom."

When a bud was getting ready to form a grape, the foxes would come in and take it out and the fruit would never be produced. Using beautiful language, the lovers are saying, "Let's identify and work through the things that will undermine our love." While the foxes can represent many things in a relationship, I think one of the things they represent is unforgiveness. A small grievance may not seem like much, but when it's left unresolved it can run wild and destroy a marriage.

That's one reason I think catching the little foxes, those moments of unforgiveness, are so important to a healthy relationship. Now, just like a small fox, you may be tempted to think of a grievance as no big deal or not worth your time. But the strongest marriages learn how to deal with the tiniest of foxes and embrace a lifestyle of forgiveness.

When it comes to anger, there is no greater antidote than forgiveness. When you choose to forgive, not only do you set the other person free, but you also become free yourself. The ability to forgive is one of God's most amazing gifts; and in your marriage, you have the opportunity to practice forgiveness every day.

How would you respond to the following statements? Mark your response on the graph below each question.

I find it's easy to forgive anyone and everyone.

1    2    3    4    (5)    6    7    8    9    10

Strongly disagree                                    Strongly agree

I find that it's easier to forgive some people than others even if they've committed the same offense.

1    2    3    4    5    6    7    8    (9)    10

Strongly disagree                                    Strongly agree

It's easier to forgive my spouse for some things but much harder to forgive for others.

1    2    3    4    5    6    (7)    8    9    10

Strongly disagree                                    Strongly agree

When I reflect on my past, I can think of several people I still have not forgiven.

1    2    (3)    4    5    6    7    8    9    10

Strongly disagree                                    Strongly agree

Some things are just beyond forgiveness.

(1)    2    3    4    5    6    7    8    9    10

Strongly disagree                                    Strongly agree

# Introduction to DVD

Every marriage has conflict and issues that need to be worked through. The question is, How do you and your spouse respond when conflict arises? Do you find yourself offering forgiveness and moving on? Or do you find yourself harboring unspoken resentment and anger? No matter what you've been through in your marriage, you can learn to forgive and let go. In the process, you'll find your marriage growing into something more wonderful than you can imagine. In this third lesson, we'll discover what the Bible says about forgiveness and how to guard your marriage from any foxes. Let's watch as Gary and Ted introduce you to this lesson.

# Discussion and Study

One of the foundations of being a forgiving person is recognizing just how much you have been forgiven. That's one reason the Scriptures make it so clear that God offers forgiveness for sins.

On the chart below, draw lines connecting the Scriptures with the promises of God.

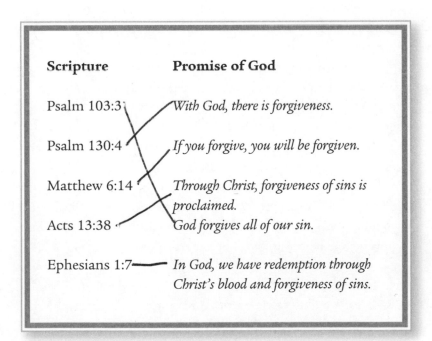

| Scripture | Promise of God |
|-----------|----------------|
| Psalm 103:3 | *With God, there is forgiveness.* |
| Psalm 130:4 | *If you forgive, you will be forgiven.* |
| Matthew 6:14 | *Through Christ, forgiveness of sins is proclaimed.* |
| Acts 13:38 | *God forgives all of our sin.* |
| Ephesians 1:7 | *In God, we have redemption through Christ's blood and forgiveness of sins.* |

When you recognize just how much you've been forgiven, it becomes easier to forgive others. When you experience grace and mercy, you are better able to extend them to others.

Take a few moments to think about just how much God has forgiven you. In what ways have you seen God pursue a relationship with you despite your sins, weaknesses and shortcomings?

_Through captive time, relationships, Song, other people. fellowship, Church_

## The Nature of Forgiveness

Forgiveness is more than just letting a grudge go. Real forgiveness happens not just when we don't harbor anger or resentment but when we actually move toward wanting to bless the other person. One of the best definitions of forgiveness I've ever heard is simply this: *Forgiveness is me giving up the right to hurt you for hurting me. But better, I want to help you, not get even.*

In the Sermon on the Mount, Jesus tackles the issue of forgiveness and nurturing a forgiving spirit with a challenging command. Read Matthew 5:39-42:

> But I tell you, Do not resist an evil person. If someone strikes you on the right cheek, turn to him the other also. And if someone wants to sue you and take your tunic, let him have your cloak as well. If someone forces you to go one mile, go with him two miles. Give to the one who asks you, and do not turn away from the one who wants to borrow from you.

Jesus recounts a variety of situations that would naturally evoke the anger. Yet Jesus makes it clear not to respond with anger. What does Jesus encourage followers to respond with instead?

Have you ever tried following this command in your own life? Describe a specific situation.

_____

_____

_____

_____

In what ways is this passage particularly true in a marriage?

_you should humble youreself to your_

_____

_____

_____

What does it mean for you to turn your cheek, offer your tunic or walk two miles with your spouse?

_____

_____

_____

_____

What's intriguing is that Jesus doesn't stop there! He continues as He explains how forgiveness is meant to be a way of life. And that forgiveness includes doing things for—not against—those who harm you. Read Matthew 5:43-48.

> You have heard that it was said, "Love your neighbor and hate your enemy." But I tell you: Love your enemies and pray for those who persecute you, that you may be sons of your Father in heaven. He causes his sun to rise on the evil and the good, and sends rain on the righteous and the unrighteous. If you love those who love you, what reward will you get? Are not even the tax collectors doing that? And if you greet only your brothers, what are you doing more than others? Do not even pagans do that? Be perfect, therefore, as your heavenly Father is perfect.

What does Jesus want all of us to do for our enemies? Do you think these commands hold true within a marriage? Explain.

*Love them, yes your spouse may feel like an enemy for a split second.*

If you really embrace a spirit of forgiveness, there are three essential elements to keep in mind.

## 1. Forgiveness Has No Limits

No matter what has happened in your marriage, you cannot place any limits on your forgiveness. Real forgiveness does not have requirements or contingencies. It is freely given, not earned.

This principle was clearly demonstrated through the life of Jesus Christ. After horrific abuse on the way to His crucifixion, Jesus still prayed for His abusers.

Read Luke 23:34. What is Jesus' response to those who are cruel to Him?

*Ask God to forgive the people that tortured him.*

Many times we try to put conditions on our forgiveness. Statements that begin with "I'll forgive you if . . ." fill our minds and hearts. Can you think of any "I'll forgive you if . . ." statements that have slipped into your marriage? Explain.

Remember that forgiveness is not conditional. It's given freely just as Christ forgives us. When you forgive, you are able to experience peace, love and grace in renewed measure. Have you ever thought about the fact that the quality of your life hinges on your ability to forgive with no limits? What do you need to let go of that you have been holding on to?

_____

_____

_____

_____

In what ways have you seen the quality of a person's life decrease with unforgiveness?

_____

_____

_____

_____

Have you ever seen someone take unforgiveness to the grave? Describe. What was the result?

_My Dad_____

_____

_____

_____

## 2. Forgiveness Means No Remembrance of Sin

When you truly forgive, you give up the right to repeatedly bring up a situation or hold a grudge. You truly let it go, never to take hold of it again. Did you know that's what God does with our sin when we ask for forgiveness?

Read Psalm 103:12. What can be learned about forgiveness from the way God forgives?

_Infinite forgiveness_____

_____

_____

_____

_____

First Corinthians 13:5 says that love "keeps no record of wrongs suffered." In other words, love means not keeping track of someone's failures. Do you think it's possible to truly forgive apart from love? Why or why not?

*Not possible without love*

_____

_____

_____

_____

Do you find it difficult to let go of keeping track when you feel like you've been wronged in your marriage? Explain.

_____

_____

_____

_____

_____

What steps do you need to take to erase the tally board of wrongs in your mind?

_____

_____

_____

_____

## 3. Forgiveness Means Letting Go Completely

You can justify a lot of reasons within your own mind not to forgive or not to forgive completely. One biblical man who had a laundry list of reasons to harbor resentment and bitterness was Esau. His younger brother, Jacob, took Esau's birthright in a moment of weakness, and took Esau's father's blessing in a moment of trickery. Yet years later, we get a rich portrait of forgiveness when Jacob and Esau's paths cross.

Read Genesis 33:1-11. What was Esau's reaction to seeing his brother? (See vv. 4-5.)

_____

_____

_____

_____

How did his reaction demonstrate forgiveness?

_____

_____

_____

What did Jacob do to win the trust and affection of his brother? (See vv. 1-3,11.)

_____

_____

_____

_____

As you reflect on your relationship with your spouse, can you think of anything you're holding back in anger or unforgiveness? If so, spend some time in prayer considering the work God may want to do in your life, heart and attitude.

## Taking It with You

Forgiveness is more than just not holding something against someone. Real forgiveness means giving up any rights to retaliation and actually desiring to help the person instead of causing hurt.

As you embrace a spirit of forgiveness, it's important to remember that forgiveness has no limits. It cannot be contained. And it keeps no record of wrong. Real forgiveness lets go fully and wholeheartedly. Yet when you forgive, you become freer yourself. Forgiveness is the key to keeping short accounts and, better yet, a zero balance when it comes to being wronged in a marriage. When you forgive, you can more fully love your spouse and yourself.

# Put It into Practice

Choose at least one of these suggested activities to complete over the next week. Consider sharing with your friends or small-group members the impact it has on you and your relationship with your spouse.

## 1. Take the Forgiveness Survey

Check out pages 146-149 of *From Anger to Intimacy*.

Did anything surprise you about your responses to the test?

_____

_____

_____

_____

Did anything surprise you about your spouse's responses?

_____

_____

_____

How does taking the Forgiveness Survey help you better understand yourself? Understand your spouse?

_____

_____

_____

_____

## 2. Take Time to Pray

Pull out a blank sheet of paper and ask God to reveal any areas of unforgiveness in your life. After recording each one, prayerfully consider how the unforgiveness has hurt your own heart and marriage. Ask God to forgive you for harboring resentment, anger and any bitterness. Then spend time praying for and blessing your spouse.

## 3. Hide the Word in Your Heart

This week commit to memorize at least three Scriptures. Several are suggested below, but feel free to choose your own.

> If my people, who are called by my name, will humble them-selves and pray and seek my face and turn from their wicked ways, then will I hear from heaven and will forgive their sin and will heal their land (2 Chronicles 7:14).

> Help us, O God our Savior, for the glory of your name; deliver us and forgive our sins for your name's sake (Psalm 79:9).

> You have heard that it was said, "Love your neighbor and hate your enemy." But I tell you: Love your enemies and pray for those who persecute you, that you may be sons of your Father in heaven. He causes his sun to rise on the evil and the good, and sends rain on the righteous and the unrighteous (Matthew 5:43-45).

# Crafting the Perfect Apology

Chapter 7 in *From Anger to Intimacy*

I'd love to tell you that I'm the perfect husband. I come home from work every day with a smile on my face, fresh flowers in hand and ready to fulfill every one of my wife's wishes. But the truth is that I'm far from perfect. There are moments when my wife asks me to run an errand after work, and on the way home, I forget. There are those mornings when my wife asks me to do a chore, and I get distracted playing with the kids or watching television. And there are those conversations when she tells me we have dinner plans and somehow the conversation slips away and I end up double-booking us.

In those instances, I have learned that nothing is more effective for our relationship than a well-crafted apology. That means using fresh phrases and not just resorting to the familiar "Sorry." That means looking her in the eye and talking to her about my mistake. That means taking personal responsibility and acknowledging that it was my fault. And that means asking for forgiveness in a meaningful way. When I do those things, I'm amazed at how quickly our relationship is restored to one of peace, joy and love.

One of the most amazing things about learning to craft the perfect apology is that it comes in handy in every relationship. The fact is that all of us make mistakes, forget what we've agreed to do and miscommunicate from time to time. When we learn to apologize, and do it well, we can strengthen all of our relationships, especially our marriage.

When was the last time you made a mistake and needed to apologize to someone? How did it go?

_____

_____

_____

_____

Can you think of a time when you apologized to someone and it didn't go well? What did you say? What was your tone and body language? What did you leave unspoken?

_____

_____

_____

_____

What has been the most meaningful apology someone has ever given to you? Describe.

_____

_____

_____

_____

_____

# Introduction to DVD

Every marriage has its challenging moments. After a conflict, it's important to know how to ask for forgiveness. A good apology can go a long way to restoring health to a relationship. You may be tempted to think that an apology is saying that you're sorry, but a great apology is so much more. It incorporates your words, your tone of voice and your body language. Let's watch as Gary and Ted teach you how to craft the perfect apology.

# Discussion and Study

A well-crafted apology is not just a good idea, it's also a biblical idea. But please recognize that apologizing is not for the faint of heart. It's not always easy, but it will allow you to grow and mature as a follower of Christ.

One important aspect of apologizing is that it forces you to take personal responsibility for something that you or your spouse may have misunderstood. That means you can't hide or play games. You can't wear a mask, insisting that everything is fine. And you can't wait until the other person apologizes. Instead, a well-crafted apology is an opportunity to grow in humility and grace.

Read Romans 12:18: "If possible, as far as it depends on you, live at peace with everyone." Why is a well-crafted apology important to abiding by this verse?

_____

_____

_____

_____

_____

Read 2 Corinthians 5:18. What ministry is every believer called to? Why is a well-crafted apology important to fulfilling this ministry?

_____

_____

_____

_____

_____

It's important to note that we are only reconciled to God as far as we are reconciled to each other. That's why we can't have a great relationship with God if our relationships with each other are sour. God's design for your marriage is that you will live in peace and harmony no matter what storms of life may come.

There are five tools you need in order to craft the perfect apology.

## Tool 1: Put Some Thought into It

The best apologies aren't usually spur-of-the-moment words. They take time to think through. When you consider an apology, think about what you've done and need to own up to. Think about the remorse you feel. Identify the harm you caused. And consider the very best time and situation to offer the apology. Sometimes timing is everything.

One man who put some thought into his apology is found in the parable of the prodigal son. A young man asks for his share of his father's inheritance and heads off on his own. After he hits rock bottom, he realizes that his life would be better if he was a servant of his father. But before he heads home, he puts some thought into his apology.

Read Luke 15:11-32. What does the son plan to say to his father? (See vv. 18-19.)

_____

_____

_____

_____

_____

_____

What makes this a well-crafted apology?

_____

_____

_____

_____

_____

Does the son get the opportunity to offer the apology? Why or why not?

_____

_____

_____

_____

_____

Even if you do not get the opportunity to deliver your apology, why is it important to craft one? How does it help you and your relationship with God?

_____

_____

_____

_____

_____

## Tool 2: Focus on Feelings, Not Issues

One of the reasons that it's important to focus on feelings instead of issues is that attention to the issues often leads to more tension and disagreement. Most people feel hurt not about an issue as much as an attitude or a harsh word from someone else.

When you focus on the feelings, then you can identify when or where you went wrong or crossed a line. And you have the opportunity to gently remind that person that no issue is worth losing a relationship over.

Read Matthew 9:9-13. What was Jesus criticized for in this passage?

_____

_____

_____

_____

_____

What was Jesus' response? (See vv. 12-13.)

_____

_____

_____

_____

_____

Why do you think Jesus desires compassion so much?

_____

_____

_____

_____

_____

What role does compassion play in offering a well-crafted apology?

_____

_____

_____

_____

_____

## Tool 3: Become a Great Wordsmith

Offering a great apology means using well-selected words. That may mean thinking of fresh phrases to use or even buying a dictionary in order to find the words that best describe what you're trying to say. When you become a great wordsmith, you can better articulate what's on your heart and in your mind.

Read Psalm 19:14. Why are the words you choose so important in an apology?

_____

_____

_____

_____

Read Ephesians 4:29. How can paying attention to the words you use every day help prevent the need to apologize?

_____

_____

_____

_____

Why is it important to prayerfully consider what you're going to say when apologizing?

_____

_____

_____

_____

_____

## Tool 4: Remember that Less Is Often More

Sometimes when we give an apology it's easy to get tongue-tied or, worse, start talking and not stop. When that happens, you can actually undermine your own apology by bringing up hurtful memories or saying something that causes further damage to the relationship. That's why the best apologies are short and focused.

Read Proverbs 10:19. How does the wisdom of this verse apply to crafting an apology?

_____

_____

_____

Read Proverbs 13:3. How does the wisdom of this verse apply to crafting an apology?

_____

_____

_____

Read Proverbs 17:27. How does the wisdom of this verse apply to crafting an apology?

_____

_____

_____

Read Proverbs 21:23. How does the wisdom of this verse apply to crafting an apology?

_____

_____

_____

_____

## Tool 5: Whenever Possible, Apologize in Person

In our modern world, it's easy to use technology to apologize. Whether you write a text message or an email, post on someone's blog or leave a message on someone's cell phone, there are lots of opportunities to offer apologies that are not face to face. But the most meaningful apologies always come when you can look someone in the eye and talk to him or her directly. In those moments, the person gets to listen to your tone, read your body posture and see the sincerity in your eyes.

While there are some situations and circumstances when it's not possible to apologize in person, take advantage of any chances when you can. Not only will it mean more to the other person, but it will also allow you to grow as an individual so that you can offer the perfect apology—one that leads to the restoration and health of the relationship. That means that you need to take the initiative.

Read Matthew 5:23-24. Why do you think Jesus instructs us to be reconciled to one another before we give? What does this passage reveal about the importance of relationships?

_____

_____

_____

_____

_____

## The Rich Rewards

Whether you realize it or not, a good apology goes a long way to making peace among people. This is true not only in your own relationships;

peace spreads as others learn from you what a well-crafted apology looks and sounds like.

Read Matthew 5:9. What reward is promised to the peacemakers?

_____

_____

_____

_____

Read James 3:13-18. How does a well-crafted apology help you grow into who God has called you to become?

_____

_____

_____

_____

## Learn How to Accept an Apology

Learning to craft the perfect apology will go a long way to helping your marriage and other relationships. But in addition to offering a good apology, it's also important to know how to accept an apology and forgive those who have hurt you.

One of the most moving accounts of forgiveness is demonstrated in the story of Joseph. After his brothers threw him into a well to die, he was later taken out and sold into slavery. His life included a series of highs and lows all because of the act of his brothers. Many years later, he meets his brothers again, but they do not recognize him. When he finally reveals his identity, he embraces them with love and forgiveness.

Read Genesis 45:1-15. What encouraging words does Joseph offer his brothers? (See v. 5.) How does saying these things free his brothers from the guilt they were probably feeling?

_____

_____

_____

_____

In the midst of the situation, who does Joseph keep his focus on? (See v. 8.) In the midst of being wronged, who should you keep your focus on?

_____

_____

_____

_____

What does Joseph bless his brothers and father with? (See vv. 10-11.)

_____

_____

_____

_____

What physical response does Joseph use to express love and care for his brothers? (See vv. 14-15.) Why is a hug or appropriate physical contact important when accepting an apology?

_____

_____

_____

_____

## Taking It with You

Knowing how to craft the perfect apology gives you one of the tools you need to fulfill the call to the ministry of reconciliation that God has on your life. You are called to live at peace with all people. A great apology can go a long way to strengthening your relationships—especially your marriage relationship. When you think about what you want to say, choose your words wisely, stay focused on the feelings, stay succinct and apologize in person. You can renew and restore your relationships. When practiced within a marriage, you'll find that a well-crafted apology leads to healing and peace within the relationship.

# Put It into Practice

Choose at least one of these suggested activities to complete over the next week. Consider sharing with your friends or small-group members the impact it has on you and your relationship with your spouse.

## 1. Write a Letter of Apology

One great way to practice crafting the perfect apology is to write out what you want to say. Spend some time prayerfully considering people in your life who may have been angered or upset by something you did. Maybe there's a coworker or family member or even your own spouse. Write out a thoughtful, meaningful apology. Then, let it sit for a day and reread it the next day. What do you need to add? Delete? You may even want to have a friend read it for a fresh perspective. Then, if possible, consider reading the letter to the person you may have offended. If you cannot get face-to-face time with the person, then place it in the mail. Remember that crafting the perfect apology takes time and practice. But every step goes a long way to renewing your relationships.

## 2. Hide the Word in Your Heart

This week commit to memorize at least three verses of Scripture. Several are suggested below, but feel free to choose your own.

> A man of knowledge uses words with restraint, and a man of understanding is even-tempered (Proverbs 17:27).

> Therefore if you are presenting your offering at the altar, and there remember that your brother has something against you, leave your offering there before the altar and go; first be reconciled to your brother, and then come and present your offering (Matthew 5:23-24).

> For where you have envy and selfish ambition, there you find disorder and every evil practice. But the wisdom that comes from heaven is first of all pure; then peace-loving, considerate, submissive, full of mercy and good fruit, impartial and sincere.

Peacemakers who sow in peace raise a harvest of righteousness (James 3:16-18).

## 3. Apologize to the One You Love

In a marriage, it's easy to fall into the habit of pointing a finger at your spouse and what he/she may have done or left undone. But looking at yourself helps keep a healthy perspective. Take some time over the next week to prayerfully consider some of the mistakes you may have made in your marriage. Are there any attitudes or actions that you need to apologize for? If so, take this opportunity to craft an apology and ask your spouse for forgiveness.

# Roadblocks to Forgiveness

### Chapter 8 in *From Anger to Intimacy*

There are so many misconceptions and myths about forgiveness. One of my favorites is that all you have to do when someone hurts or offends you is forgive and forget. While that sounds easy to do, it's a lot harder than you might expect!

I (Gary) recently heard about a woman who was reminded of an offense that was done to her many years before. A friend pressed her about the issue when she said, "Doesn't that just eat you alive? Aren't you still mad?" She said, "No, I distinctly remember forgetting that even happened."

The truth is that forgiving is not just forgetting that something happened or, worse, pretending like it never happened at all. Real forgiveness requires letting go of the offense even if it still pops up in your memory from time to time. Real forgiveness also means handing over the situation to God and trusting Him with all the details. When you truly forgive, you place yourself in a position where you can respond to God rather than react to people or situations.

I know that in my own relationship with my wife, Norma, there are moments when I get upset. She may make plans without communicating with me, or more often than not, I make the plans without communicating with her! These moments can lead to frustration, tension and even a flare-up of anger. But when I take a step back to understand what has really happened, take responsibility for my actions and attitudes and let go of the offense, I am freer to love and honor her. The result is that our relationship grows stronger and deeper, and an even greater level of security and trust develops in our marriage.

Think about a recent offense involving your spouse. How long did it take you to forgive your spouse? What prevented you from forgiving your spouse more quickly?

_____

_____

_____

_____

_____

_____

How often are you tempted to remember previous offenses when you get upset with your spouse? Do you tend to focus on the issue at hand or bring up situations where it's happened in the past?

_____

_____

_____

_____

_____

What roadblocks do you have in your life when it comes to forgiveness?

_____

_____

_____

_____

_____

# Introduction to DVD

Forgiving someone who has truly offended or hurt you isn't always easy. As a result, you may have deposits of anger and unforgiveness in your heart from things that happened in the past. The good news is that it's never too late to rid yourself of them. No matter what anyone has done to you or what they may have left undone, you can still forgive them through the power of God's strength and grace. In the upcoming video, you'll begin to understand the roadblocks that may be standing in your way if you've been living a lifestyle of unforgiveness. Let's watch Gary and Ted discuss this important issue.

# Discussion and Study

There are nine roadblocks that can get in the way of forgiving others. As you learn to move beyond these roadblocks, you'll find that your marriage is transformed.

## Roadblock 1: Selfishness

Selfishness is a primary roadblock to forgiveness. When you're focused only on your emotions, feelings and desires, it's impossible to look outward to the needs and concerns of others. That's why it's important to be generous, rather than selfish, when it comes to forgiving others.

Read James 4:1. According to this passage, what is the source of conflicts and quarrels?

_____

_____

_____

_____

_____

_____

Read Hebrews 12:1. What encouragement does this verse contain for those who are struggling with selfishness and their fallen nature?

_____

_____

_____

_____

_____

_____

Read Colossians 2:1-3. In what way does selfishness and unforgiveness undermine all that God has for you?

_____

_____

_____

_____

## Roadblock 2: Pride

Pride is another critical roadblock to forgiveness. Pride will keep you from humbling yourself enough to ask for forgiveness or accept it from someone who offers it. That's one reason pride is so harmful—it holds us back from the redemption and restoration God has for us!

In the parable of the Pharisee and the tax gatherer, Jesus tells the story of two men with very different attitudes about themselves.

Read Luke 18:9-14. What is the difference between the two men's attitudes toward themselves? Toward God?

_____

_____

_____

_____

Which man's attitude is most representative of your own? Explain.

_____

_____

_____

_____

Why is it important to know your own faults and failures? How does knowing your own imperfections help you give more grace to others? To your spouse?

_____

_____

_____

_____

## Roadblock 3: Insecurity

Insecurity is a roadblock to forgiveness. If you do not know who you are in Christ, or you have not experienced the forgiveness of Christ, how can you extend forgiveness to others? One of the root causes of insecurity is fear. When you're insecure, thoughts like *You don't measure up, you can never do enough* and *you'll never be good enough* shape your attitudes, actions and behavior.

Yet these thoughts and beliefs are far from God's call and plan for your life. First John 4:18 says that mature love casts out all fear. In other words, when you are saturated in God's love there is no room or place for fear of any kind. You can walk with confidence and assurance of who God has made you to be. As you mature spiritually in the love of God, you'll discover that your marriage is growing stronger and your bond of love is going deeper.

On the chart below, draw lines connecting the Scriptures with the promises of God.

| Scripture | Promise of God |
|---|---|
| Psalm 34:18 | *I am your Father, and I love you even as I love my son, Jesus.* |
| Psalm 71:6 | *As a shepherd carries a lamb, I have carried you close to my heart.* |
| Isaiah 40:11 | *I can do more than you can possibly imagine.* |
| John 17:23 | *When you are brokenhearted, I am close to you.* |
| Ephesians 3:20 | *I brought you forth on the day you were born.* |

## Roadblock 4: Resentment

Resentment is a huge roadblock to forgiveness. When you begin to replay those thoughts in your mind and you focus in on what someone has done to you, you can get to the point where you want vengeance.

Jesus went out of His way on the Sermon on the Mount to say that this is no way to live. It will literally choke the life out of you. In Matthew 5, Jesus says, "You have heard that it was said to the people long ago, 'Do not murder, and anyone who murders will be subject to judgment.'" Those in the crowd recognized this teaching of the rabbis. They knew it was based on Scripture. But interestingly, Jesus didn't stop there. He went on to say, "But I tell you that anyone who is angry with his brother will be subject to judgment" (Matthew 5:22).

Jesus was saying, if you call someone an idiot, you are in danger of being brought before the court; and if you curse someone, you are in danger of the fires of hell. All too often, we like to look at the commands and make sure that we are okay with the biggies. We like to say, "I don't curse or take the name of the Lord in vain." Or, like the singsong adage, "I don't smoke, I don't chew; and I don't go with girls that do." Jesus didn't want us to only examine our hearts when it came to the large issues. He knew that you don't just wake up one morning and murder someone. It starts with the seed of resentment that sprouts into unforgiveness and anger.

Murder is a dramatic sin, and you may feel like you could never do anything like that. But the truth is, you can—because murder starts in the heart when you begin to allow those seeds of resentment and anger to go unchecked and unresolved. Resentment and unresolved anger are like drinking poison and hoping the other person gets sick; but all the while it's killing you.

Read Colossians 3:12-17. Make a list of the activities in this passage that will help you guard against resentment.

_____

_____

_____

_____

_____

Which of these are you currently practicing? Which of these do you
need to be practicing?

_____

_____

_____

_____

_____

_____

_____

## Roadblock 5: Unresolved Anger

One day, Robert Redford was walking out of a hotel room, walking
toward the elevator. The doors opened, he stepped in and a lady came
chasing after him, looked in and said, "Are you the real Robert
Redford?" Like a scene from a movie, Robert Redford said, "Only when
I'm alone." The elevator doors closed.

I love that story because it highlights the fact that we are truly ourselves when we are alone. In those moments when we are not tempted to
pretend or put on a show, we can see what's truly in our hearts. When
you're alone, you may find yourself wrestling with unresolved anger.
This is a roadblock to forgiveness and something God wants to help you
work through and heal.

I (Gary) am not into behavior modification. I don't want to change
your behaviors. I don't want to change the way you look or the way you
act. God does that. When we allow God to do the work in us and work
through the knots of unforgiveness in our lives, it changes our hearts.
And when our hearts change, everything changes, including our behavior, attitudes and actions.

We look at the outward appearance, but God looks at the heart.
That's why it's so important to be honest about any areas of unresolved anger with God and yourself. When you learn to forgive, you experience true change.

Not only can you learn to forgive, but you can also help others
along their journey.

Read Matthew 5:23-24. Why do you think it's important to be a person who asks for forgiveness?

_____

_____

_____

_____

Think of a time when you were the first in a relationship to bring up an issue and ask for forgiveness. What was the response?

_____

_____

_____

_____

Why do you think Jesus makes it clear that we are to both ask for forgiveness and extend forgiveness to those who ask?

_____

_____

_____

_____

I love the stories of people who have stopped in the middle of a church service, gotten up and left to go make things right with someone. We have a couple in our church that has been reconciled because he got up out of this church and went to another church where he knew she was. He said to himself, "I'm going to stop right now so I can go and make things right." The fruit of that decision is still blossoming in their marriage today.

## Roadblock 6: Inability to Recognize Weaknesses and Mistakes

The Bible says, "Settle matters quickly with your adversary who is taking you to court. Do it while you are still with him on the way, or he may hand you over to the judge, and the judge may hand you over to the officer, and you may be thrown into prison. I tell you the truth, you will not get out until you have paid the last penny" (Matthew 5:25-26).

We want this study to go right to the heart. We want you to begin to inventory the areas of your life that need change. You may say you have been a follower of Jesus for years, but if you have a sibling you haven't talked to since going through a family inheritance mess, then there's some work that still needs to be done. We want you to be honest about your struggles.

An important aspect of forgiving others is recognizing your own weaknesses, faults and mistakes. When you take time to recognize your own brokenness, then you are better able to extend grace and forgiveness to others who are less than perfect.

All too often, I (Gary) will hear someone rehearse his or her spouse's weaknesses. One of the most common lines I'll hear is, "But, Gary, you don't know her (or him)." The truth is that I don't need to know him or her. I need you to know yourself, and I need you to recognize that you're a work in progress too.

When you walk in humility, then you can make every effort as far as it depends on you to be reconciled to the other person.

In the book of Revelation, John finds himself in prison on the island of Patmos. In this place, God uses John to write a letter—a book of the Bible—that would influence believers for centuries to come.

Read Revelation 1:9. In this passage, how does John describe himself?

_____

_____

_____

_____

_____

How does this description make him more accessible to those who will read his writings?

_____

_____

_____

_____

_____

Why is it so important to recognize our own struggles and weaknesses?

_____

_____

_____

_____

## Roadblock 7: Misunderstanding Forgiveness

Two of the greatest myths regarding forgiveness in a marriage are:

1. If I can change the other person, or if he (she) will stop hurting me, I'll be happier.

2. If only I can change my circumstances (more money, bigger house, nicer car, etc.), I would be more likely to experience more happiness.

Which of these two myths are you tempted to believe? Why?

_____

_____

_____

_____

Which of these two myths is your spouse tempted to believe? Why?

_____

_____

_____

How does believing these myths undermine your marriage? Your ability to forgive?

_____

_____

_____

_____

## Roadblock 8: Fear of Condoning the Offense

Did you know that you can offer forgiveness without condoning an offense? Jesus demonstrated this principle time and again throughout His earthly ministry.

Read John 8:1-11. What was the offense of the woman?

_____

_____

_____

_____

_____

_____

What was the response of the teachers of the law and the Pharisees?

_____

_____

_____

_____

_____

_____

How was Jesus' response different from that of the teachers of the law and the Pharisees?

_____

_____

_____

_____

_____

_____

How did Jesus offer forgiveness without condoning the offense? (See v. 11.)

_____

_____

_____

_____

_____

How can you offer forgiveness without condoning the offenses in your marriage?

_____

_____

_____

_____

## Roadblock 9: The Passage of Time

You may be tempted to think that too much time has passed to truly forgive someone. But forgiveness has no time limits.

Imagine for a moment a table fully set. What is on the table represents all of your offenses toward your spouse. Now imagine wiping everything off the table and onto the floor in one big sweeping motion. Sometimes forgiveness is like that. We brush it all away. But over time, we begin picking up certain items off the floor. We place them back on the table where we are reminded of them and at times even use them against our spouse.

Real forgiveness means knowing that it's never too late to clear the table. That means living with a spirit of forgiveness no matter what may appear on the table.

No matter how much time has passed since an offense, make every effort to resolve it. Sit down and talk things out. If you can't have face-to-face time, then consider writing a letter or picking up the phone. Never let unforgiveness get the best of you.

Is there anyone in your past that you still need to forgive? Explain.

_____

_____

_____

_____

_____

_____

_____

Is there anyone in your present—including mother- and father-in-law, siblings and even your spouse—that you need to forgive? Explain.

_____

_____

_____

_____

_____

_____

Remember, time heals nothing. It's what you do with time that matters!

# Taking It with You

Many issues can stand in the way of truly forgiving, but with God's help, grace, strength and wisdom, you can overcome every last one. You do not need to let the roadblocks to forgiveness get the best of you. Instead, choose to forgive. Don't allow resentment, time, pride, selfishness or anything else stand in the way. When practiced within a marriage, you'll find that forgiveness is something you can offer to everyone, and then all of your relationships will be strengthened because of it.

# Put It into Practice

## 1. Removing the Roadblocks

Take a few moments to reflect on the nine roadblocks listed in this session. Which roadblock are you most prone to stumble over? What do you need to do to become more intentional about overcoming them? Prayerfully consider how you can make the changes necessary in your life to embrace forgiveness as a lifestyle.

## 2. Hiding the Word in Your Heart

This week commit to memorize at least three Scripture verses. Here are some suggestions, but feel free to choose your own.

Create in me a pure heart, O God, and renew a steadfast spirit within me. Do not cast me from your presence or take your Holy Spirit from me. Restore to me the joy of your salvation and grant me a willing spirit, to sustain me (Psalm 51:10-12).

For I will forgive their wickedness and will remember their sins no more (Hebrews 8:12).

If you see the donkey of one who hates you fallen down under its load, do not leave it there; be sure you help him with it (Exodus 23:5).

## 3. Bless Others

Think of at least two people you have had a hard time forgiving. This week do a simple act of kindness for each one. Send flowers. Give a gift. Offer an encouraging word. You can even do something anonymously. Extend kindness to those who have hurt you. Then watch for the change in your own heart.

# Forgiving the Difficult, Addicted or Cheating Spouse

### Chapters 9-12 in *From Anger to Intimacy*

Some things may seem beyond forgiveness, but the truth is that nothing is beyond God's redemption and forgiveness. No matter what your spouse has done, and no matter how difficult your spouse may seem, you can forgive. It comes down to choice.

And it's a choice that you have to make in your own heart. When it comes to unforgiveness, it's easy to point a finger, particularly if your spouse has done something terribly wrong. Yet holding on to unforgiveness actually hurts you more than it could possibly hurt the other person. You will never travel very far down the road to restoration and healing without forgiveness.

Now some of you have never been able to forgive, and the unforgiveness has deep roots in your past. Perhaps you were hurt by an adult when you were a young child. What was done against you was criminal, and you have never been able to let it go. Now that unforgiveness is compounding in your marriage. Or perhaps the source of unforgiveness is something your spouse has done that left you feeling betrayed, hurt and angry. No matter what has happened to you, you can choose to forgive and move forward in your life and all of your relationships. Even if you're tempted to think it's impossible, we're here to tell you that nothing is impossible for God!

Think of the most offensive thing someone has done against you. What emotions arise inside of you when you think about that moment?

_____

_____

_____

_____

_____

Why do you think that it's so important to forgive those who have offended you?

_____

_____

_____

_____

_____

Think of a time when you truly forgave someone for something terrible the person had done. How did the other person change as a result? How did you change?

_____

_____

_____

_____

_____

# Introduction to DVD

Unfortunately, sexual addiction and affairs are becoming an ever-increasing crisis in the church today. Men and women are losing their homes, families and jobs because of it. Some are even going to jail as a result of sexual addiction. Often sexual sins are some of the hardest to forgive because of their personal nature and the sense of betrayal that accompanies them. Yet no matter what your spouse has done or what you've done, forgiveness is available through the power of Jesus Christ. Let's watch Gary and Ted discuss this important issue.

# Discussion and Study

In this session, we want to highlight some of the practical key concepts you will need to know in order to forgive a difficult spouse. Here are four keys to forgiving a difficult spouse no matter what your partner may have done or left undone.

## Fight Your Own Attitude of Retaliation Instead of the Other Person

In the space below, write out Leviticus 19:18.

_____

_____

_____

_____

In the space below, write out Proverbs 24:29.

_____

_____

_____

In the space below, write out Romans 12:17.

_____

_____

_____

Why do you think revenge or retaliation is forbidden by God?

_____

_____

_____

_____

What harm comes of revenge or retaliation? How does it hurt you?
Other people? Future generations?

_____

_____

_____

_____

_____

_____

## Recognize that You Can't Change the Behavior of the Other Person

This is probably one of the hardest lessons of all. But no matter what
you do and no matter how much you say, you cannot change the behavior of the other person. You are 100 percent responsible for *your* actions, not the other person's actions.

The good news is that as a child of God, you do have one very powerful activity that you can do that will impact your spouse: *prayer*.
When you faithfully pray, you literally invite the power of God to move mountains in your life and marriage.

Write out John 14:12-14 below.

_____

_____

_____

_____

_____

_____

How does this verse encourage you to pray for your spouse? Those who
are difficult to get along with?

_____

_____

_____

_____

_____

Mark 11:20-25 describes Jesus' lesson from His encounter with a fig tree. He drew rich lessons on prayer and forgiveness. Read the following:

> In the morning, as they went along, they saw the fig tree withered from the roots. Peter remembered and said to Jesus, "Rabbi, look! The fig tree you cursed has withered!" "Have faith in God," Jesus answered. "I tell you the truth, if anyone says to this mountain, 'Go, throw yourself into the sea,' and does not doubt in his heart but believes that what he says will happen, it will be done for him. Therefore I tell you, whatever you ask for in prayer, believe that you have received it, and it will be yours. And when you stand praying, if you hold anything against anyone, forgive him, so that your Father in heaven may forgive you your sins."

Why is prayer the most powerful tool you have to change your marriage? Yourself?

_____

_____

_____

_____

## Love Unconditionally

Unconditional love is crucial to truly moving forward in the forgiveness God has for you! What is unconditional love? It's choosing to love rather than allow seeds of bitterness and anger take root in your heart. Now that doesn't mean you condone a wrong or sin, but it does mean that you choose not to use that event or action against the person.

Read 1 Thessalonians 4:9. According to this passage, who is the teacher when it comes to love?

_____

_____

_____

_____

Do you think it's possible to know real love apart from God? Why or why not?

_____

_____

_____

_____

_____

Who in your life has best shown or taught you about unconditional love? What did that person do or say? What did that person leave un-done or unspoken?

_____

_____

_____

_____

_____

Read 1 Corinthians 13. In the space below, make a list of each of the de-scriptions of love. Which of them are hardest for you to follow? Which of them come most naturally?

_____

_____

_____

_____

_____

_____

> _"Anger is like an ember that never goes out. It may look like it's lying dormant, but when the right circumstances come along, it flames up. Knowing that there's something there—an ember of anger—but being unable to identify the exact source undermines trust in a relationship. Before you know it, intimacy wanes. Communication shuts down. Distance becomes the new norm."_

## Respond to God, Not to Man

When you get upset with your spouse, it's easy to react and unleash your emotions, especially when your buttons are being pushed. But as a child of God, you are asked to mature beyond that fleshly response. You are invited to lift your eyes off of your spouse and place them on God so that you can get a clearer perspective and have a more healthy, life-giving response.

---

*"Tommy Nelson, pastor of Denton Bible Church, says that if you habitually harbor unforgiveness in your heart, you need to call your faith into question. That may seem harsh, but your ability to love and forgive is based on the love and forgiveness you have received from God. If you can't forgive people of their offenses, then you have to ask yourself the tough question, Where am I in relationship to the Lord?"*

---

Read 1 Chronicles 29:12. What strengths of God are listed in this passage?

_____

_____

_____

_____

_____

What is God truly your source of? What do you turn to Him for? In what areas do you try to depend on yourself?

_____

_____

_____

_____

_____

_____

Read Psalm 68:35. What does God give to His people? Which of the items listed in this passage have you received from God? Explain.

_____

_____

_____

_____

## Saying No to Temptation

All of us struggle with temptations. One common struggle is lust. Do you know what I (Gary) am doing to try to solve the lust issue in my life? When I see someone who catches my eye, I think, *Good job, God.* Instead of letting the temptation turn to lust (remember, temptation is not sin), I start wondering if her dad loves her. I wonder if she is dressing that way to get attention because she never had a dad that gave her attention. (I have counseled with enough people in the last couple of years to see how this stuff works.) I wonder if it is because she doesn't feel very secure about herself that she is going to show herself to every man she sees. I wonder if her husband is nice to her. I wonder if her husband really loves her. Let me tell you that when you get in that mode and you start praying for that person, it is hard to jump into thoughts of lust.

I find that God gives me the strength and grace to overcome temptation! Grace is given in abundance to the humble. When I recognize my need for God and the reality that I am spiritually bankrupt apart from Him, then I am in a position to cry out for Him and wait expectantly for His response. I know with confidence that as God's child, He wants me to experience the fullness of His kingdom, which includes "righteousness, joy and peace in the Holy Spirit" (Romans 14:17-18).

Do you realize that no one is beyond temptation? From the opening pages of Genesis, we get portraits of humanity facing temptation. Consider the following passage:

Now the serpent was more crafty than any of the wild animals the LORD God had made. He said to the woman, "Did God really say, 'You must not eat from any tree in the garden'?" The woman said to the serpent, "We may eat fruit from the trees in the garden, but God did say, 'You must not eat fruit from the tree that is in the middle of the garden, and you must not touch it, or you will die.'" "You will not surely die," the serpent said to the woman. "For God knows that when you eat of it your eyes will be opened, and you will be like God, knowing good and evil" (Genesis 3:1-5).

What deception did the serpent use to trick Eve?

_____

_____

_____

_____

_____

Why do you think Eve fell for the temptation?

_____

_____

_____

_____

The serpent is described as "more crafty than any of the wild animals." In what ways does temptation prey on your weaknesses?

_____

_____

_____

_____

_____

Even Jesus was tempted while He was on Earth. Read Matthew 4:1-11. Who tempted Jesus? (See v. 1.)

_____

_____

_____

_____

What was Jesus' response to each temptation? What did Jesus use to defend Himself?

_____

_____

_____

_____

_____

How can you use the defensive shield that Jesus used?

_____

_____

_____

_____

_____

What are you doing right now in your life to store up God's Word in your heart?

_____

_____

_____

_____

_____

## Dealing with Sexual Addiction

Sexual addiction and cheating can blindside you and your marriage. But they are not reasons to give up on your marriage. We know of too many couples who through counseling, prayer and an attitude of humility have been able to discover healing and restoration. Here are three things to keep in mind if you discover that your spouse has a sexual addiction or has had an extramarital affair.

First, it's important that you do not take the blame. If you find yourself in a relationship where your spouse is dealing with an addiction, it's important for you to realize that you are not responsible for your spouse's actions. He or she is completely responsible. Now that does not mean that you are completely absolved of making changes in your behavior or attitude to give your mate the best possible chance for overcoming the addiction; but the addiction or affair is not your fault.

Second, you need to make a conscious choice to forgive. You may be tempted to think that your spouse has crossed the line into the land of "impossible to forgive." But the truth is that there is no such place! Sexual addiction or cheating is not on the list of sins not to forgive. It is hurtful and harmful, no doubt, but it is also forgivable. As a follower of Jesus Christ, you are required to forgive. Even if your spouse does not change his or her behavior or attitude, you are still called to forgive. Remember, forgiveness has nothing to do with whether or not your spouse changes, but has everything to do with you and your relationship with God.

---

*"Forgiveness is the antidote to anger. In fact, the word 'forgiveness' in Greek is actually two words put together meaning 'being released' and 'being pardoned.' When we release someone from an offense and pardon them, then we become freer ourselves."*

---

Finally, you need to make every effort to assist your spouse on the journey to recovery. While this process isn't easy, it is rewarding. When you commit to helping your spouse overcome an addiction or weakness without taking responsibility for causing it, then you are in the best position to prayerfully support, encourage and bring out the best in your spouse. Simple activities like finding qualified, biblically based counselors, making time to heal your own emotions and frequent prayer can go a long way to restoring a fallen spouse.

## The Most Common Question

Here is one of the most common questions we are asked:

When is it permissible to leave him (or her)?

That is a tough question. We do not believe that addiction to pornography is a legitimate, biblical reason to divorce your mate. Instead, we would encourage a spouse to create space for a while until a plan for restoration and healing is in place. We always look for every possible way to save a marriage.

If you are ready to end your marriage over a sexual addiction or extramarital affair, we would encourage you to prayerfully consider the situation. Here is a simple test to see if you and your mate are serious about recovery.

1. Is the behavior relentless? Is there a charge-ahead, egotistical attitude toward the addiction? Explain.

2. Is the behavior persistent? Is there an "I ain't stoppin'" attitude? Explain.

3. Is he or she unrepentant? Is there an "I'm doing nothing wrong" attitude? Explain.

# Taking It with You

No matter what has happened in your marriage, it's never too late to fight to save your relationship. Forgiving a moral failure or addiction is challenging, but it's not a challenge that's impossible to overcome. Remember, you are 100 percent responsible for your actions, not the actions of your spouse. That means that you have the freedom to choose to forgive. It's not an easy decision, and it does not condone the behavior or action. But it will set you free to love and trust again and experience the healing and restoration that only come from knowing God.

# Put It into Practice

## 1. Be Supportive

If you have been through the devastation of an affair or a spouse with an addiction, look for specific ways to support him (her) during the path to healing. If you know someone who has experienced this kind of loss and pain, look for ways to be a voice of encouragement and hope in their life.

## 2. Hide the Word in Your Heart

This week commit to memorize at least three verses of Scripture. Several are suggested below, but feel free to choose your own.

> The LORD is compassionate and gracious, slow to anger, abounding in love. He will not always accuse, nor will he harbor his anger forever; he does not treat us as our sins deserve or repay us according to our iniquities. For as high as the heavens are above the earth, so great is his love for those who fear him; as far as the east is from the west, so far has he removed our transgressions from us. As a father has compassion on his children, so the LORD has compassion on those who fear him (Psalm 103:8-13).

> O LORD, you have searched me and you know me. You know when I sit and when I rise; you perceive my thoughts from afar. You discern my going out and my lying down; you are familiar with all my ways. Before a word is on my tongue you know it completely, O LORD (Psalm 139:1-4).

> Therefore if anyone is in Christ, he is a new creature; the old has gone, the new has come! (2 Corinthians 5:17).

## 3. Reflect on Your Notes Throughout This Study

As you near the end of this study, read through your various responses and entries. Are there any Scriptures that particularly challenged or captured your heart? What has God been trying to speak to your heart through this study? How have you been challenged? Share your responses with your spouse.

# From ANGER to INTIMACY

## Leader's Guide

# Anger: Stuff, Spew or Study

Chapters 1–2 in *From Anger to Intimacy*

---

This session will explore the three outlets of anger:
stuffing, spewing and studying.

## For Starters Discussion Questions

*Think of several small things that people do that get on your nerves. In the space below, make a list of three pet peeves.* Answers will vary and include everything from bad drivers to spouses who leave their dishes in the sink. This question is designed to highlight the unique ways every individual is annoyed and become more sensitive to them.

*Now take a moment to study the pet peeves you listed. Why do those specific things bother you? Is there a history or background story to why they are bothersome? Explain.* Answers will vary. This question is designed to help participants recognize the reasons that particular things become pet peeves. Often the small things that bother us trace back to our childhood and upbringing or bad experiences in life.

*How does listening to your spouse's pet peeves and the reasons behind them, and your spouse's listening to your pet peeves, help you both feel more understood? Why is understanding each other so important for a healthy relationship?* Answers will vary, but hopefully understanding each other's pet peeves will make spouses more sensitive and willing to avoid bothersome behavior.

## Discussion and Study

*Can you think of any situation in which anger is a healthy response?* Social injustice or the oppression of humans often stirs a righteous anger. Though we can be very right in the reasons for our anger, we can also be very wrong in the way we express that anger.

*Read Nehemiah 5:1-6. What was the situation that made Nehemiah angry?* The poor were being oppressed and abused.

*What did his emotional response cause Nehemiah to do? (See Nehemiah 5:7-11.)* Nehemiah was angry, but his anger led to action that would stop the oppression.

*What was the outcome of Nehemiah's righteous response? (See Nehemiah 5:11-13.)* The people were given back their land with nothing more demanded of them according to the leaders.

*Why do you think some of these emotions are more likely to lead you to anger than others?* Answers will vary. Everyone is wired differently.

*How can recognizing these hot spots in your emotional life help you prevent yourself from becoming angry?* Answers will vary, but this question is designed to make participants think proactively about how they can get a handle on the anger in their life.

*Are there any other emotions not listed that lead you to anger? If so, explain.* Answers will vary.

*Read Genesis 4:4-5. What was the Lord's response to each of the offerings?* The Lord looked with favor on Abel and his offering, but on Cain and his offering He did not look with favor.

*According to Genesis 4:5, what was Cain's emotional response to the situation?* He was angry.

*Reflecting on the list of Primary Emotions (Sources) that Lead to Anger, which ones do you think Cain experienced or felt?* Answers will vary.

*What is the Lord's response and encouragement to Cain? (See Genesis 4:7.)* "If you do what is right, will you not be accepted? But if you do not do what is right, sin is crouching at your door; it desires to have you, but you must master it."

*What can be learned about dealing with anger from Genesis 4:6?* It affects you more than you realize. For Cain, it affected his "face," or countenance.

*Unfortunately, anger got the best of Cain. What did Cain do in Genesis 4:8?* Cain attacked and killed his brother.

*In what ways in your own life have you seen anger lead to "death"?* Answers will vary.

*In what ways have you seen this pattern manifest itself in your own life?* Answers will vary.

*What processes or steps do you currently have in place that allow you to be angry without sinning?* Answers will vary but may include things like taking a deep breath before responding, taking a time-out, asking for a better time to discuss the issue, or other options.

*Reflecting on this list, which of these are hot buttons for you? Which of these are hot buttons for your spouse?* Answers will vary.

*Do you or your spouse have a hot button that is not listed above? If so, explain.* Answers will vary.

*Read Ephesians 4:26. In what ways does this verse specifically address those who are prone to stuffing?* The verse instructs us not to let the sun go down on our anger. Don't hold it inside.

*What advice does the verse give on dealing with anger?* Don't let a single day pass without dealing with your anger issues.

*In what ways have you found this verse to offer wisdom and truth into your own life?* Answers will vary.

*In what ways is this verse particularly vital to the health of a marriage relationship?* Answers will vary.

*Read Proverbs 29:22. In what ways have you seen this verse apply in your own life? Your marriage? Your workplace?* Answers will vary.

*Read Daniel 3:7-23. What are the names of the three men who refused to bow? (See Daniel 3:12.)* Shadrach, Meshach and Abednego.

*What was King Nebuchadnezzar's attitude when he learned of the three men? (See Daniel 3:13,19.)* He was furious.

*Do you think King Nebuchadnezzar is best described as a stuffer, a spewer or a studier of anger? Why?* Answers may vary, but King Nebuchadnezzar was a spewer because he took out his aggression by trying to kill the three servants of God.

*How did the three men who did not bow down respond to King Nebuchadnezzar's anger in Daniel 3:16-18?* They were confident and held their ground based on their faith, but they didn't retaliate or respond in anger.

*In what ways was the response of the three men in Daniel 3:16-18 a model of how to respond when you are faced with an angry person?* They respected their accuser. They answered with wisdom, grace and strength in the face of a stressful situation.

*Read Acts 7:54-60. What was the response of the listeners to Stephen's words? (See Acts 7:54,57-58.)* They were furious and gnashed their teeth at him. They all rushed at him, dragged him out of the city and began to stone him.

*What was Stephen focused on during this difficult time? (See Acts 7:55-56.)* He was focused on God. He had an audience of One.

*What was Stephen's response to the anger being spewed verbally and physically? (See Acts 7:60.)* He responded, "Lord, do not hold this sin against them." He was forgiving and gracious until his death.

# Personal Responsibility and Emotions

Chapters 3–5 in *From Anger to Intimacy*

---

This session is designed to explore the hot button
issues of most couples and highlight ways
that men and women can nurture their emotions,
resulting in a healthy marriage.

## For Starters Discussion Questions

*On a scale of 1 to 10, how important is it for you to feel connected to your spouse?*
Answers will vary, but this question is designed to highlight what's truly
important for each partner in a marriage.

*On a scale of 1 to 10, how important is it for you not to feel controlled by your
spouse?* Answers will vary, but this question is designed to highlight
what's truly important for each partner in a marriage.

*What attitudes, actions and behaviors undermine your ability to establish connect-
edness? What steps do you need to make to change?* Answers will vary, but participants should look for specific ways to strengthen their marriage and
avoid undermining behavior.

## Discussion and Study

*Consider the following patterns that can lead to an anger response. As you read through this progression, can you identify a scenario in your own marriage that starts with hurt, progresses to want and fear, and results in anger?*

1. **You hurt.** *A wide range of emotions surface whenever you are wounded, including anger, confusion, worry, rage, frustration, horror and embarrassment. These can often feed off of each other and lead to more anger.*

2. **You want.** *When you're hurt, you want to find a solution that will fix the situation and make you feel better. The result is unmet expectations. You may think, "If only my spouse would (fill in the blank)." Anytime you put your expectations for help in the wrong place, you will be disappointed, fueling the hurt and anger.*

3. **You fear.** *Whenever a conflict causes powerful emotions of hurt, it stirs specific fears. You may fear that you're not smart enough, competent enough, attractive enough or good enough. The fear only fuels the cycle of anger.*

4. **You react.** *In order to handle a situation, you fall into well-worn patterns of reacting when someone pushes one of your fear buttons. Rather than base your reactions in love, they are found in an unhealthy pattern of response that often fuels more anger into a situation.*

Answers will vary, but responses highlight the sources of anger for individuals. Recognizing the source is important to finding a solution.

*Read James 1:19-20. What specific instruction is given in this passage regarding the response time to a situation?* Everyone should be quick to listen, slow to speak and slow to become angry. We should take time before responding.

*Read Proverbs 21:23. In what ways have you found this verse to be true in your marriage?* Answers will vary.

*Read Proverbs 14:17. What are some of the dangers of being quick-tempered rather than self-controlled?* You'll make foolish mistakes and people will not like you. You'll undermine your relationships and push people away.

*Read Psalm 70. What is David's request to God regarding his enemies? (See Psalm 70:1-3.)* "May those who seek my life be put to shame and confusion; may all who desire my ruin be turned back in disgrace. May those who say to me, 'Aha! Aha!' turn back because of their shame."

*What is David's request to God for those who are faithful? (See Psalm 70:4.)* "But may all who seek you rejoice and be glad in you; may those who love your salvation always say, 'Let God be exalted!'"

*What is David's request to God regarding himself in Psalm 70:5?* "Yet I am poor and needy; come quickly to me, O God. You are my help and my deliverer; O Lord, do not delay." David seeks God's help in the situation. He does not take matters into his own hands.

*Why do you think it was important for David to cry out to God in these moments rather than take matters into his own hands? How are the psalms a reminder to you to cry out to God, no matter the situation?* David is able to keep a clean heart and avoid sinning by turning to God and trusting Him with the matter. The psalms are a wonderful reminder that we can be completely transparent with the God who knows us better than we know ourselves.

*Read Matthew 18:32-34. What was the outcome of the story?* In anger his master turned him over to the jailers to be tortured until he should pay back all he owed.

*Read Matthew 18:35. Why did Jesus tell this story? What message was He trying to convey?* Jesus taught the followers that this is how His heavenly Father will treat each of them unless they forgive their brother from their heart. In other words, He wanted His disciples to get the link between the idea that just as you have been freely forgiven as God's children, so you are to freely forgive others.

*How does knowing how much you have been forgiven by God help you extend forgiveness to others? To your spouse?* Answers will vary, but as children of God, we are called to give away that which we have been given and in the process reflect the goodness of God to others.

*According to John 13:2-3, what was already happening in Judas' heart?* The devil had already prompted Judas Iscariot, son of Simon, to betray Jesus.

*Though Jesus could have been angry with Judas, how does Jesus respond to Judas and all of the disciples? (See John 13:1-11.)* Jesus serves Judas by washing his feet even though He knew the disciple would betray Him. He also washed the feet of the others—knowing they would leave Him alone in His darkest hour.

*In what ways is Jesus' response surprising or unexpected?* Instead of responding with anger, Jesus responds with love and service.

*Read John 13:12-17. What are Jesus' specific instructions?* "Now that I, your Lord and Teacher, have washed your feet, you also should wash one another's feet. I have set you an example that you should do as I have done for you."

*How does serving and loving one another diffuse anger within a marriage?* Answers will vary.

*What is your emotional reaction to being served and loved unconditionally?* Answers will vary.

*Read Ephesians 4:2. In what ways does abiding by this verse help create a judgment-free zone?* When you are completely humble, gentle, patient and you bear with one another in love, it creates an atmosphere of security where you can tackle any issue together.

*What steps can you take in your own marriage to create a judgment-free zone?* Answers may vary. Affirming one another. Praying together. Showing gratitude. Expressing physical affection. Overlooking small grievances. Keeping short accounts about upsetting moments. These and many other things can go a long way to helping create and maintain a judgment-free zone.

*Read Philippians 4:8-9. What does this passage encourage us to focus our hearts and minds on? How does focusing on these things change your attitude, actions and perspective?* "Whatever is true, whatever is noble, whatever is right, whatever is pure, whatever is lovely, whatever is admirable—if anything is excellent or praiseworthy—think about such things." Focusing on these things cannot help but change the way you react and respond to others.

*Read Psalm 119:11. What is one of the direct benefits of storing up God's Word in your heart?* You sin less.

*Read Colossians 3:16. What are some practical ways that you can incorporate the reading of Scripture, praise and worship into your everyday life?* Answers will vary.

*Read 2 Corinthians 10:3-5. What are the "strongholds" listed in this passage? (See 2 Corinthians 10:4.)* "Arguments and every pretension that sets itself up against the knowledge of God."

*How have you seen these "strongholds" try to take hold in your own thought life? In your marriage?* Answers will vary.

*Why is it important to get rid of any bitterness, resentment or anger before it takes root in your life?* When you nip it in the bud stage, you don't have to allow it to grow in you.

*Read Luke 8:43-49. What did the woman do to Jesus? Why do you think she did it?* She touched the edge of Jesus' cloak for healing.

*What was Jesus' response? (See Luke 8:45-46.)* He sought to identify and acknowledge her.

*How did the woman take personal responsibility for her actions? (See Luke 8:47.)* She admitted her action.

*What was Jesus' response to her taking responsibility? (See Luke 8:48.)* He told her she was healed and told her to go in peace.

*Can you think of a time when you took personal responsibility and found that God met you in a special way at that place? If so, describe.* Answers will vary.

*In this story, Jesus' final words to the woman are simply, "Go in peace." In what ways does taking responsibility invite peace into your life?* Answers will vary.

*Read John 13:1. How is God's love expressed in this verse?* Jesus was going to give up His life for the redemption of God's people.

*Read John 15:9. What invitation is issued regarding the love of God?* "As the Father has loved me, so have I loved you. Now remain in my love."

*Read John 14:27. What gift does Jesus offer in this verse?* Peace.

*Read Philippians 4:7. What role can the peace of God play in your life?* God's peace guards your heart and mind.

*Read Hebrews 11:1. How are hope and faith fused?* It's impossible to have faith without hope. They go hand in hand.

*Read 1 Corinthians 13:7. How are hope and love fused?* Part of loving others is having hope for them.

*Read 1 Corinthians 13:1-3. Why is bathing your words in love so important?* Without love, words mean nothing and can even become annoying.

*Read Galatians 5:22-23. How can this be a grid for the words you speak to your spouse?* Each of the ideas listed in this passage is something to consider before speaking to your spouse. Do your words show these things?

If not, think hard before saying them, or preferably change the way you express yourself.

*Read Hebrews 12:6-11. What is the purpose of godly discipline in your life? (See Hebrews 12:7-8.)* We become children of God and reflect our Father's character and attributes.

*What are some of the fruit or benefits of being disciplined by God? (See Hebrews 12:10-11.)* We become holy, producing a harvest of righteousness.

*Read 2 Corinthians 12:9-10. Why did Paul boast in his weaknesses?* Because he wanted all glory to go to God.

*What was accomplished through such boasting?* He reminded others of his own imperfections, struggles and weaknesses.

*How does being honest about your weaknesses and faults help you connect with your spouse better?* It makes you easier to relate to and more accessible. When you're not trying to be perfect, people are more likely to feel connected to you and relate to the transformation going on in your life and heart.

# The Spirit of Forgiveness

### Chapter 6 in *From Anger to Intimacy*

This session explores the idea that when it comes to anger, there is no greater antidote than forgiveness. The ability to forgive is one of God's most amazing gifts, and you have the opportunity to practice forgiveness every day.

## For Starters Discussion Questions

*How would you respond to the following statements? Mark your response on the graph below each question.* Answers will vary among participants and are designed to help people recognize areas of unforgiveness.

## Discussion and Study

*On the chart below, draw lines connecting the Scriptures with the promises of God.*

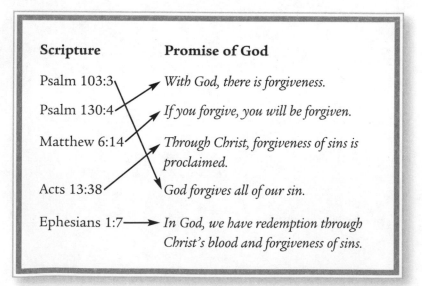

| Scripture | Promise of God |
|---|---|
| Psalm 103:3 | *With God, there is forgiveness.* |
| Psalm 130:4 | *If you forgive, you will be forgiven.* |
| Matthew 6:14 | *Through Christ, forgiveness of sins is proclaimed.* |
| Acts 13:38 | *God forgives all of our sin.* |
| Ephesians 1:7 | *In God, we have redemption through Christ's blood and forgiveness of sins.* |

*Take a few moments to think about just how much God has forgiven you. In what ways have you seen God pursue a relationship with you despite your sins, weaknesses and shortcomings?* Answers will vary.

*Jesus recounts a variety of situations that would naturally evoke anger. Yet Jesus makes it clear not to respond with anger. What does Jesus encourage followers to respond with instead?* Kindness and generosity.

*Have you ever tried following this command in your own life? Describe a specific situation.* Answers will vary.

*In what ways is this passage particularly true in a marriage?* When we respond with kindness and generosity in our marriage, we create an atmosphere of honor and security in the relationship that fosters a lifestyle of forgiveness.

*What does it mean for you to turn your cheek, offer your tunic or walk two miles with your spouse?* Answers will vary, but they should be specific to each marriage.

*What does Jesus want all of us to do for our enemies? Do you think these commands hold true within a marriage? Explain.* Love your enemies. Yes—this is particularly true in marriage when the relationship hits difficult spots.

*Read Luke 23:34. What is Jesus' response to those who are cruel to Him?* He prays for them and asks God to forgive them.

*Many times we try to put conditions on our forgiveness. Statements that begin with "I'll forgive you if . . ." fill our minds and hearts. Can you think of any "I'll forgive you if . . ." statements that have slipped into your own marriage? Explain.* Answers will vary.

*Have you ever thought about the fact that the quality of your life hinges on your ability to forgive with no limits?* Answers and responses will vary.

*In what ways have you seen the quality of a person's life decrease with unforgiveness?* Answers will vary, but participants should offer specific examples, preferably without using names if in a group gathering.

*Have you ever seen someone take unforgiveness to the grave? Describe. What was the result?* Answers will vary, but participants should offer specific examples, preferably without using names if in a group gathering.

*Read Psalm 103:12. What can be learned about forgiveness from the way God forgives?* Just as the distance between east and west cannot be measured, so we should go to the greatest possible lengths to forgive others.

*First Corinthians 13:5 says that love "keeps no record of wrongs" suffered. In other words, love means not keeping track of someone's failures. Do you think it's possible to truly forgive apart from love? Why or why not?* Answers will vary.

*Do you find it difficult to let go of keeping track when you feel like you've been wronged in your marriage? Explain.* Answers will vary.

*What steps do you need to take to erase the tally board of wrongs in your mind?* Answers will vary.

*Read Genesis 33:1-11. What was Esau's reaction to seeing his brother? (See Genesis 33:4-5.)* Esau embraced his brother, kissed him and wept.

*How did his reaction demonstrate forgiveness?* His physical affection toward his brother was a reflection of the affection and forgiveness that had taken place in his own heart.

*What did Jacob do to win the trust and affection of his brother? (See Genesis 33:1-3,11.)* He attempted to win his brother's trust and affection through gifts and generosity.

# Crafting the Perfect Apology

Chapter 7 in *From Anger to Intimacy*

---

This session looks at the power of a well-crafted apology
in renewing and restoring a broken relationship.

## For Starters Discussion Questions

*When was the last time you made a mistake and needed to apologize to someone?*
*How did it go?* Answers will vary, but they should highlight the idea that
all of us need to apologize from time to time.

*Can you think of a time when you apologized to someone and it didn't go well?*
*What did you say? What was your tone and body language? What did you leave*
*unspoken?* Answers will vary.

*What has been the most meaningful apology someone has ever given to you?*
*Describe.* Answers will vary, but pay attention to the details of what
made the apology truly meaningful. These are clues and hints for crafting your own meaningful apology.

## Discussion and Study

*Read Romans 12:18. Why is a well-crafted apology important to abiding by this*
*verse?* Because apologies are necessary in life. All of us make mistakes.
But a meaningful apology goes a long way to restoring a relationship.

*Read 2 Corinthians 5:18. What ministry is every believer called to? Why is a well-crafted apology important to fulfilling this ministry?* Every believer is called to the ministry of reconciliation, and apologies are essential to restoring broken relationships.

*Read Luke 15:11-32. What does the son plan to say to his father? (See Luke 15:18-19.)* "Father, I have sinned against heaven and against you. I am no longer worthy to be called your son; make me like one of your hired men."

*What makes this a well-crafted apology?* The son takes ownership for his mistakes. He humbles himself. He asks for mercy and has a repentant attitude.

*Does the son get the opportunity to offer the apology? Why or why not?* No, the son didn't get to offer the apology because the father was waiting with open arms to accept him.

*Even if you do not get the opportunity to deliver your apology, why is it important to craft one? How does it help you and your relationship with God?* Because you never know how the other person will respond. The practice of crafting a meaningful apology provides the opportunity to take personal responsibility for what you've done and prayerfully consider what you've learned through it.

*Read Matthew 9:9-13. What was Jesus criticized for in this passage?* Eating with tax collectors and sinners.

*What was Jesus' response? (See Matthew 9:12-13.)* Jesus said, "It is not the healthy who need a doctor, but the sick. But go and learn what this means: 'I desire mercy, not sacrifice.' For I have not come to call the righteous, but sinners." Jesus responds firmly but with graciousness, not ill-will.

*Why do you think Jesus desires compassion so much?* Answers will vary, but Jesus desires compassion because our God is compassionate. When we are compassionate, we reflect this attribute of God to the world around us.

*What role does compassion play in offering a well-crafted apology?* Compassion makes an apology more genuine.

*Read Psalm 19:14. Why are the words you choose so important in an apology?* Because they should be pleasing to God first, and then pleasing to the other person second.

*Read Ephesians 4:29. How can paying attention to the words you use every day help prevent the need to apologize?* When you avoid unwholesome talk, you can avoid many hurt feelings, anger, slander and dissension.

*Why is it important to prayerfully consider what you're going to say when apologizing?* Because God wants to empower you to be a minister of reconciliation. He wants to give you the wisdom and grace to restore the relationship.

*Read Proverbs 10:19. How does the wisdom of this verse apply to crafting an apology?* Too many words can get you in trouble.

*Read Proverbs 13:3. How does the wisdom of this verse apply to crafting an apology?* Thinking ahead about what you want to say can help protect you and the relationship.

*Read Proverbs 17:27. How does the wisdom of this verse apply to crafting an apology?* Remaining calm and even-tempered is important when delivering an apology.

*Read Proverbs 21:23. How does the wisdom of this verse apply to crafting an apology?* Choosing your words wisely can prevent further ruin of the relationship.

*Read Matthew 5:23-24. Why do you think Jesus instructs us to be reconciled to one another before we give? What does this passage reveal about the importance of relationships?* Jesus wants His believers to love one another more than just give offerings. Relationships are extremely important. Through our godly relationships, we represent God and His work to the world around us.

*Read Matthew 5:9. What reward is promised to the peacemakers?* They will be called sons of God.

*Read James 3:13-18. How does a well-crafted apology help you grow into who God has called you to become?* Well-crafted apologies are essential to being peacemakers in God's kingdom.

*Read Genesis 45:1-15. What encouraging words does Joseph offer his brothers? (See Genesis 45:5.) How does saying these things free his brothers from the guilt they may be feeling?* Joseph reminds his brothers that God was with him and went before him all along the way. He reminds them of God's goodness and favor, and removes their guilt.

*In the midst of the situation, who does Joseph keep his focus on? (See Genesis 45:8.) In the midst of being wronged, who should you keep your focus on?* Joseph focuses on God, just as we should!

*What does Joseph bless his brothers and father with? (See Genesis 45:10-11.)* A safe place to live and food.

*What physical response does Joseph use to express love and care for his brothers? (See Genesis 45:14-15.) Why is a hug or appropriate physical contact important when accepting an apology?* Joseph hugged, embraced and wept. His physical touch was an assurance of the love and forgiveness he felt in his heart.

# Roadblocks to Forgiveness

## Chapter 8 in *From Anger to Intimacy*

This session is designed to help participants
break through some of the roadblocks in their way
when it comes to truly forgiving.

### For Starters Discussion Questions

*Think about a recent offense involving your spouse. How long did it take you to forgive your spouse? What prevented you from forgiving your spouse more quickly?*
Answers will vary.

*How often are you tempted to remember previous offenses when you get upset with your spouse? Do you tend to focus on the issue at hand or bring up situations where it's happened in the past?* Answers will vary.

*What roadblocks do you have in your own life when it comes to forgiveness?*
Answers will vary but may include things like something done that seems unforgivable, time or the fact that the person is no longer accessible.

*Read James 4:1. According to this passage, what is the source of conflicts and quarrels?* Desires that battle within you.

*Read Hebrews 12:1. What encouragement does this verse contain for those who are struggling with selfishness and their fallen nature?* We are surrounded by a cloud of witnesses. Many who have gone before us faced similar struggles but overcame. So can we!

*Read Colossians 2:1-3. In what way does selfishness and unforgiveness undermine all that God has for you?* It separates us from fellow believers who need to experience the riches of the fullness of God.

*Read Luke 18:9-14. What is the difference between the two men's attitudes toward themselves? Toward God?* One refused to take responsibility for his actions and saw himself as perfect. The other man acknowledged his faults and flaws and genuinely asked for forgiveness.

*Which man's attitude is most representative of your own? Explain.* Answers will vary.

*Why is it important to know your own faults and failures? How does knowing your own imperfections help you give more grace to others? To your spouse?* Knowing your own faults and failures keeps you humble and dependent on God. It also helps you look beyond small grievances and weaknesses of others in the name of love.

*On the chart below, draw lines connecting the Scriptures with the promises of God.*

| Scripture | Promise of God |
|---|---|
| Psalm 34:18 | *I am your Father, and I love you even as I love my son, Jesus.* |
| Psalm 71:6 | *As a shepherd carries a lamb, I have carried you close to my heart.* |
| Isaiah 40:11 | *I can do more than you can possibly imagine.* |
| John 17:23 | *When you are brokenhearted, I am close to you.* |
| Ephesians 3:20 | *I brought you forth on the day you were born.* |

*Read Colossians 3:12-17. Make a list of the activities in this passage that will help you guard against resentment.* Clothe yourselves with compassion, kindness, humility, gentleness and patience. Bear with each other. Forgive grievances. Put on love. Let the peace of Christ rule in your hearts. Be thankful. Teach and admonish one another with all wisdom. Sing psalms, hymns and spiritual songs with gratitude in your hearts to God. Do it all in the name of the Lord Jesus, giving thanks to God.

*Which of these are you currently practicing? Which of these do you need to begin practicing?* Answers will vary.

*Read Matthew 5:23-24. Why do you think it's important to be a person who asks for forgiveness?* Because God calls you to the ministry of reconciliation—whether or not you are the one harboring the anger or unforgiveness.

*Think of a time when you were the first in a relationship to bring up an issue and ask for forgiveness. What was the response?* Answers will vary.

*Why do you think Jesus makes it clear that we are to both ask for forgiveness and extend forgiveness to those who ask?* So that we can receive God's forgiveness.

*Read Revelation 1:9. According to this passage, how does John describe himself?* A companion in the suffering.

*How does this description make him more accessible to those who will read his writings?* We recognize his humanity—that he was no different from any of us.

*Why is it so important to recognize our own struggles and weaknesses?* Accessibility and humility develop as we are honest with our struggles.

*If I can change another person, or if they'll stop hurting me, I'll be happier. If only I can change my circumstances (more money, bigger house, nicer car, etc.), I would be more likely to experience more happiness. Which of these two myths are you tempted to believe? Why?* Answers will vary.

*Which of these two myths is your spouse tempted to believe? Why?* Answers will vary.

*How does believing these myths undermine your marriage? Your ability to forgive?* They short-circuit the work God wants to do in your relationship.

*Read John 8:1-11. What was the offense of the woman?* She was caught in the act of adultery.

*What was the response of the teachers of the law and Pharisees?* They wanted to stone her.

*How was Jesus' response different from that of the teachers of the law and the Pharisees?* He used the opportunity to show that all of us have sinned and fall short of the glory of God.

*How did Jesus offer forgiveness without condoning the offense? (See John 8:11.)* He told her to go and sin no more.

*How can you offer forgiveness without condoning the offense in your marriage?* Answers will vary.

*Is there anyone in your past that you still need to forgive? Explain.* Answers will vary.

*Is there anyone in your present—including mother- and father-in-law, siblings and even your spouse—that you need to forgive? Explain.* Answers will vary.

Session 6

# Forgiving the Difficult, Addicted or Cheating Spouse

Chapters 9-12 in *From Anger to Intimacy*

---

This session challenges participants to forgive the
most difficult of offenses and help others as they seek
to restore their relationships and marriages.

### For Starters Discussion Questions

*Think of the most offensive thing someone has done against you. What emotions
arise inside of you when you think about that moment?* Answers will vary but
may include anger, bitterness, rage, fury and numbness, among others.

*Why do you think it's so important to forgive those who have offended you?*
Because if you don't forgive, you remain tied in knots over the situation,
limiting your growth and reconciliation with others and God.

*Think of a time when you truly forgave someone for something terrible the person
had done. How did the other person change as a result? How did you change?*
Answers will vary, but sometimes the only change is seen in our own
hearts. Other times, we get to be witnesses to the transforming power of
God in someone else's life.

## Discussion and Study

*In the space below, write out Leviticus 19:18.* "Do not seek revenge or bear a grudge against one of your people, but love your neighbor as yourself. I am the Lord."

*In the space below, write out Proverbs 24:29.* "Do not say, 'I'll do to him as he has done to me; I'll pay that man back for what he did.'"

*In the space below, write out Romans 12:17.* "Do not repay anyone evil for evil. Be careful to do what is right in the eyes of everybody."

*Why do you think revenge or retaliation is forbidden by God?* Because it furthers the destructive effects of sin. Also, taking things into your own hands undermines faith and the ability to trust in God.

*What harm is a result of revenge or retaliation? How does it hurt you? Other people? Future generations?* Revenge and retaliation affect and hurt more than just the two people involved—they hurt friends, neighbors and coworkers during the fall-out. Depending on the revenge or retaliation, it can affect your kids and generations to come.

*Write John 14:12-14 below.* "I tell you the truth, anyone who has faith in me will do what I have been doing. He will do even greater things than these, because I am going to the Father. And I will do whatever you ask in my name, so that the Son may bring glory to the Father. You may ask me for anything in my name, and I will do it."

*How does this verse encourage you to pray for your spouse? Those who are difficult to get along with?* Answers will vary.

*Why is prayer the most powerful tool you have to change your marriage? Yourself?* Because nothing is impossible with God, and prayer can transform your spouse and you!

*Read 1 Thessalonians 4:9. According to this passage, who is the teacher when it comes to love?* God.

*Do you think it's possible to know real love apart from God? Why or why not?* It's impossible to know real love apart from God, because God is love.

*Who in your life has best shown or taught you about unconditional love? What did that person do or say? What did that person leave undone or unspoken?* Answers will vary.

*Read 1 Corinthians 13. In the space below, make a list of each of the descriptions of love. Which of them are hardest for you to follow? Which of them come most natural to you?* "Love is patient, love is kind. It does not envy, it does not boast, it is not proud. Love is not rude, it is not self-seeking, it is not easily angered, and it keeps no record of wrongs. Love does not delight in evil but rejoices with the truth. It always protects, always trusts, always hopes, and always perseveres. Love never fails." Some of these will come more easily for different people based on their personality and upbringing.

*Read 1 Chronicles 29:12. What strengths of God are listed in this passage?* Wealth, honor, strength and power.

*What is God truly your source of? What do you turn to Him for? Where do you try to depend on yourself?* Answers will vary.

*Read Psalm 68:35. What does God give to His people in this passage? Which of the items listed in this passage have you received from God? Explain.* Power and strength.

*What deception did the serpent use to trick Eve?* The serpent twisted the truth.

*Why do you think Eve fell for the temptation?* Answers will vary, but include the idea that she did not trust God's Word; greed; pride.

*The serpent is described as "more crafty than any of the wild animals." In what ways does temptation prey on your weaknesses?* Temptation is often crafty in its approach. It seeks us out when we're tired or worn down.

*Even Jesus was tempted while He was on Earth. Read Matthew 4:1-11. Who tempted Jesus? (See Matthew 4:1.)* The devil tempted Jesus.

*What was Jesus' response to each temptation? What did Jesus use to defend Himself?* Jesus used the Word of God to defend Himself against all three temptations.

*How can you use the defensive shield that Jesus used?* Scripture is a powerful tool against temptation.

*What are you doing right now in your life to store up God's Word in your heart?* Answers will vary.

SMALLEY
*relationship*
C E N T E R

The Smalley Relationship Center provides conferences and resources for couples, singles, parents, and churches. The Center captures research, connecting to your practical needs and develops new tools for building relationships.

## resources include:

- Over 50 best-selling books on relationships
- Small Group curriculums on marriage & parenting
- Church-wide campaign series with sermon series, daily emails and much more
- Video/DVD series
- Newlywed kit and pre-marital resources

## www.garysmalley.com website includes:

- Over 300 articles on practical relationship topics
- Weekly key truths on practical issues
- Daily devotionals
- Conference dates and locations
- Special events
- Weekly newsletter
- Free personality & core fear profiles
- Request a SRC Speaker

To find out more about Gary Smalley's speaking schedule, conferences, and to receive a weekly e-letter with articles and coaching ideas on your relationships, go to www.garysmalley.com or call 1.800.8486329

Attend our live **I Promise Marriage Seminars** taught by

# DRS. GARY & GREG
# SMALLEY

A six session marriage seminar based on the new
I Promise book and Purpose Driven Curriculum

Free Resources: go to **www.garysmalley.com**

- **Weekly E-letter**

Receive articles, coaching tips and, inspirational encouragement
from Gary Smalley which will help you build a more effective and
stronger marriage.

- **Profiles** ①

The overall theme of I Promise is security, and you can take a 20 question test on how secure your most important relationship is.

(Bonus: After you take that profile consider taking our personality
profile which gives you even more insight into what kind of
personality styles you andyour spouse fall into.)

Bring a weekend of marriage miracles to YOUR CHURCH

"Our ministry designed a powerful retreat for churches taught by my co-writer and pastor, Ted Cunningham. His humor and Biblical teaching will bring a weekend of marriage miracles!"

—Gary Smalley

CONTACT US @
WWW.GARYSMALLEY.COM